REALLY?

SEARCHING FOR REALITY
IN A CONFUSING WORLD

The Keswick Year Book 2014

REALLY?
SEARCHING FOR REALITY
IN A CONFUSING WORLD

Jonathan Lamb
Chris Sinkinson
Vaughan Roberts
David Robertson
Becky Manley Pippert
Ivor Poobalan
Roger Carswell
Ian Coffey
Ruth Padilla DeBorst

First published 2015

British Library Cataloguing in Publication Data
A catalogue record for this book is available from the British Library.

ISBN: 978–1–78359–270–8

Set in Dante 12.5/16pt
Typeset in Great Britain by CRB Associates, Potterhanworth, Lincolnshire
Printed and bound in Great Britain by Ashford Colour Press Ltd, Gosport, Hampshire

Contents

The Addresses

Introduction by the Chairman of the 2014 Convention

Our theme for the 2014 Keswick Convention was: 'Really? Searching for Reality in a Confusing World'. Perhaps understandably, there were friends who, with some incredulity, asked, 'Really?' when we described our vision of a Convention which fed and strengthened the faith of committed Christians at the same time as providing opportunities for others to explore and question! In the event, however, we were delighted to see people come to faith each week and many thousands reenergized in their discipleship through the ministry of God's Word.

Our morning Bible Readings brought us a compelling exposition of the gospel through the early chapters of Romans, an exploration of how faith meets the realities of life in the Psalms, and an arresting insight into the Christian worldview through the Bible overview. Evening celebrations focused on the big questions of discipleship, through Mark's Gospel and the letter to the Philippians. As ever, the combination of biblical exposition, challenging application and heart-warming congregational worship came together to bring renewal for God's people for his mission in the world, which is always our aim at Keswick.

This Year Book will give you a taste of some of the most memorable teaching at the Convention. Alongside it, the 'Really?' Study Guide is an excellent resource to enable individuals and small groups to explore and discuss it in more depth – available online from thinkivp.com.

Alongside those who attended the Convention, thousands of others benefited from its ministry through CDs, DVDs and digital downloads. We hope that reading the Year Book will leave you wanting more. If it does, why not visit www.keswickministries.org, where you can find free downloads of the main talks, and the Essential Christian site, where you can purchase CDs and DVDs. This will extend your appreciation of Keswick's ministry and enable you to share it with others.

We hope you enjoy this reminder of Keswick 2014 and that it will lead you to the life-transforming reality of Christ in whom all grace is found for our life in a confusing world.

John Risbridger
Chair, Keswick Ministries

The Bible Readings

Reality: How Can I Make Sense of Life, the Universe and Everything?

by Jonathan Lamb

Jonathan is the CEO and minister-at-large for Keswick Ministries. For the past eleven years he has served as Director of Langham Preaching, a global programme providing training for pastors and preachers in over seventy countries around the world. He is a recent past Chairman of Keswick Ministries, and often speaks at conferences, training events and other 'Keswick' Conventions around the world. He is the author of several books, and this summer his book *Preaching Matters* is published in the Keswick Foundations series (IVP). He lives with his wife Margaret in Oxford.

Reality: How Can I Make Sense of Life, the Universe and Everything? Psalm 33

For the first time in many years of driving we have a Sat Nav in our car, and the lady with the recorded voice is now becoming a close friend. The other day I was driving to Nottingham along a newly built road and, of course, the Sat Nav showed me driving across a wheat field. The charming lady was very polite: 'In 500 metres, turn back.' I kept going. Then she seemed to become more insistent, sounding like a headmistress: 'In 200 metres, turn back . . . turn back.'

All of us have mental maps, of course, and I don't mean road navigation systems. I mean a way of looking at life which helps us to find our way, helps us understand how the world works and how we fit into it. Some people call this a 'worldview' – we assume certain things to be true, and we navigate through life according to that basic set of values, that mental map. In fact, a worldview is not just a vision *of* life, but a vision *for* life. It helps us make sense of the world around us, but it also shapes how we live; it helps us determine what really matters. It's a lens through which to look at the world and make sense of it. And a worldview needs to be able to answer our biggest questions.

Listen to this revealing comment by C. S. Lewis: 'I believe in Christianity as I believe that the sun has risen – not only because I see it, but because by it I see everything else.'[1] Lewis is saying that as we come to understand the God of the Bible, and supremely God as revealed in Jesus Christ, we are then able to see everything else in proper perspective. David said something similar in Psalm 36:9, when he spoke to God: 'In your light we see light.' Our Christian conviction is that faith in the God of the Bible, faith in Jesus Christ, provides us with a framework by which to make sense of reality. It becomes the unifying influence in our lives.

That is the theme for Keswick this year. Each morning this week we are going to look at 'Songs in the Key of Life'. The Psalms comprise 150 songs written over a period of 800 years, and here we discover a theology of the whole Bible coupled with a commentary on every aspect of our human experience. These songs are totally realistic about human life, and they matter because their teaching about life is thoroughly God-centred. They speak of God as he truly is. It's no surprise that Jesus used the Psalms in his teaching more often than any other part of the Old Testament and that, in turn, the Psalms lead us to Jesus himself.

Today we ask the question: 'What is reality?' It's one of the big questions of our age, and we find that question raised in our culture more and more – in popular science, in magazines, and in movies too. For example, movies like *The Matrix* or *The Truman Show* remind us that reality matters. We don't want to be swept along on a tide of illusion; we want to know how things really are.

What is reality? A simple answer to the question is that reality is everything that appears to our senses. But of course there are many things that are then ruled out: we can't sense an electron, but it's real enough. And in any event, that answer is not straightforward. As Morpheus said in *The Matrix*, 'If you mean [reality is] what we can taste, smell, hear and feel, then what's real is nothing more than electrical signals interpreted by your brain.'

As you can imagine, philosophers have fun with the question too. The ancient Chinese philosopher, Laozi, once asked, 'If, when I am asleep, I am a man dreaming that I am a butterfly, how do I know, when I am awake, that I am not a butterfly dreaming I am a man?'

Then, of course, there are many today who want to escape reality. There are all kinds of escapist routes, whether drug and alcohol abuse, or a fantasy holiday, or getting completely absorbed in so-called reality TV. Anything to avoid thinking about ultimate realities.

But the reason why the subject has gained prominence these days is because, for many people, the answer to the question: 'What is reality?' is this: all that exists is matter, energy, space and time – nothing else. According to our culture, we now live in a world without windows. That means this world is all there is. There is no soul, just brain chemistry; there is no spiritual world, just the physical; there is no Sovereign Creator, just blind evolutionary forces; there is no afterlife, just this present existence. So anything that claims to go beyond that must be dismissed. Christians, it is suggested, aren't living in the real world. To believe in God is actually to run away from reality; believers are delusional, seeking refuge in a toxic delusion that warps their minds.

The question is serious. As we've said, everyone needs a map that helps them to find their way, a framework for making sense of their world. Alister McGrath recently gave an example from trauma studies, which have emphasized the importance of having a sense of coherence to help victims cope with the senseless events they have been through. That is, we can manage with life and its uncertainties if we are able to see beneath the surface and grasp what really matters.

Which is what we will find as we now turn to one of the greatest poems in the Old Testament songbook, Psalm 33. It has a short introduction balanced by a short conclusion – it begins with a call to rejoice (verses 1–3), and ends with a call to hope (verses 20–22). And then in between, we're invited to sing some majestic cadences about the true God, and his involvement in the foundations of reality.

First, there is the *call to rejoice* (verses 1–3). There are five commands to sing for joy. They are strong expressions, better understood as shouts of joy and deliverance. It's robust worship – with a strong bass, blasts of trumpets, raised voices – because the psalmist is about to introduce us to a set of amazing reasons for joyful trust in God.

He points us to three foundations of reality.

1. The reality of the God who is (verses 4–5)

> For the word of the LORD is right and true;
>   he is faithful in all he does.
> The LORD loves righteousness and justice;
>   the earth is full of his unfailing love.

He begins with the reality that *God is*. It is a statement about God's word and God's character. It's interesting to see how the psalmist uses a poetic style to build his anthem. It's an example of what is called 'parallelism', where a second and then a third line add to the first, all heading in the same direction, all building to one profound statement. And it uses the most commonly used words to describe God's character and action: *truthfulness, faithfulness, righteousness, justice, steadfast love*. The psalmist affirms that God is an utterly reliable presence in this universe, and all of these qualities undergird the world he has made; they provide its moral framework. It's the first thing that we must say about reality: *God is*.

Did you notice the culmination of verse 5? It leads to the big headline: 'the earth is full of his unfailing love.' It's the pivot of the psalm, since the rest of the song unpacks its meaning in relation to the whole of space and time. I wonder if you have the unfailing love of God as the central reality of your life? God's steadfast love is fundamental to reality – it is behind his actions in creation and in his care for us and his world; it shapes his plans and purposes for us and for all things. And it is true even in bewildering moments, as we see in psalms such as Psalm 91. When she was held in Ravensbrück concentration camp, Betsie ten Boom was brave enough to say, 'He has not forgotten us.' And what convinced her? 'For as high as the heavens are above the earth, so great is his love for those who fear him' (Psalm 103:11).

God's steadfast love is the spring of his common grace for all human life, and even for how society should function. Here is Michael Wilcock's comment on this verse: 'The truth is that none of the areas of human study touched on in Psalm 33 – science, history, geography, politics – can ever be properly understood apart from this moral framework.'[2]

Already we begin to see some very significant implications. First, we notice that the psalmist doesn't set out to prove God's existence; he simply declares it. The first words of Scripture are: 'In the beginning, God', and so it is with Psalm 33. If we are to understand our world and ourselves, this is the place to begin. It sounds very obvious, but in fact it is a major dividing line in how people understand the world. Since the seventeenth century many people influenced by Western philosophy have assumed that the place to begin is not with God, but with 'I' – 'I think, therefore I am.' So I evaluate, I assess. But Psalm 33 reminds us that God is not an object to be evaluated. It simply declares: *God is*. He is the Creator who made us and, as we'll see, he is the one to whom we are accountable, *not* the other way round. It's an important shift of perspective. A recent word that has entered our global vocabulary is 'selfie' – a self-portrait taken by a digital camera, usually for posting on a social network site. The habit has taken hold around the world, and it almost implies, I am at the centre of my universe. But Psalm 33 says, reality begins with the God who is.

The second implication of verses 4 and 5 is that they declare the *moral qualities* of the God who is – righteous, true, faithful, just, loving. As we have said, these qualities are built into the foundation of creation. This is a moral universe, patterned on God's character. And it's true to life – we are aware of a moral order outside of us, to which we know we are accountable. We have a sense of what is right, and a sense of guilt when we do wrong. And there is a coherence about our world, a reliability, a truthfulness, which reflects the God who brought it into being, and that provides a pattern for all of life. True freedom for humankind, real life, can only be found when we live in line with the qualities of the God in whose image we are made.

The so-called 'New Atheism' struggles with the issue of moral order. Commenting on this, Madeleine Bunting wrote in *The Guardian* that 'our sense of morality cannot simply be explained as a product of our genetic struggle for evolutionary advantage.'[3] But Psalm 33 reminds us that there is a set of unchanging God-given moral values, and they arise from the God who is. We can speak of goodness and righteousness and justice as permanent realities because they derive from the character of the eternal God.

In summary, then, verses 4 and 5 speak of God's word, God's work and God's covenant love. As Michael Wilcock says, 'This power is not mere power.'[4] We are to see ourselves as objects of God's love, a love which has our best interest at heart, a love that shapes God's ultimate purposes and plans, a love expressed in the Christian gospel – 'God so loved the world that he gave his one and only Son' (John 3:16). 'The earth is full of his unfailing love', and we join the psalmist in longing that all men and women should experience that reality.

2. The reality of the God who speaks (verses 6–9)

If you saw the opening ceremony of the London Paralympics, you would have heard Stephen Hawking, the theoretical physicist, say these words: 'Ever since the dawn of civilization, people have craved an understanding of the underlying order of the world – why it is as it is, and why it exists at all.'

Psalm 33 answers that question at a personal and at a cosmic level:

By the word of the LORD the heavens were made,
their starry host by the breath of his mouth.
He gathers the waters of the sea into jars;
he puts the deep into storehouses.

Let all the earth fear the LORD;
   let all the people of the world revere him.
For he spoke, and it came to be;
   he commanded, and it stood firm.
(verses 6–9)

We see from the psalm that God speaks both a powerful word and a reliable word.

A powerful word

'By the word of the Lord the heavens were made . . . For he spoke, and it came to be' (verses 6, 9).

As the Bible frequently reminds us, when God speaks, things happen. In the psalm we hear echoes of Genesis 1. He spoke the words and creation came to be. Tim Keller suggests that's a good way to define power – it is the ability to bring about your wishes. Whilst here in Keswick I would like to have climbed Skiddaw before breakfast this morning, but even though I have that desire, I don't have the power to make it happen. But God is able to bring about in reality every aspect of his will and purpose. Isaiah 55 describes this powerful word that achieves God's purpose. It's like the water cycle – the rain falls, it achieves its purpose in watering the earth, and it returns. So with God's word, 'It will achieve the purpose for which I sent it' (verse 11).

The writer to the Hebrews makes it clear: 'By faith we understand that the universe was formed at God's command' (Hebrews 11:3). And it is the same in Psalm 33: 'He spoke, and it came to be' (verse 9). His word brought order out of chaos. Just a sentence or two was enough. 'By the word of the LORD the heavens were made, their starry host by the breath of his mouth' (verse 6).

It's difficult to calculate, but apparently there could be up to 400 billion stars in our galaxy, the Milky Way, which is an average-sized galaxy. There are other spiral galaxies out there with more than a trillion stars, and giant elliptical galaxies with 100 trillion stars. And there are probably more than 170 billion galaxies in the observable universe. Multiply that together and you get 10 to the power of 24 – that's a quadrillion of stars. 'Made by the breath of his mouth,' says the psalmist. Derek Kidner is right: this is why we can speak of a UNIverse, because it is the work of a single, self-consistent mind.[5] So it's no surprise that the created world is a reason for the psalmist to call us to joyful praise, to more committed trust.

In our home group we have several Oxford University academics. I might be very intimidated, except that they are true, humble believers in the same Lord. Two of them are husband and wife, Steve and Katherine. Katherine is a Professor of Astrophysics, exploring the vastness and complexity of the universe, and her husband Steve, a Professor of Physics, who studies the smallest ingredients of the universe, looking at how electrons get on with one another. And both extremes call forth our praise – from the unimaginable dimensions of the expanding universe, to the minuteness of subatomic particles with incredibly short half-lives – they each provoke our wonder and our worship. This reality also provokes a sense of awe, and it's no wonder that the psalmist speaks to all nations, to all people: 'Let all the earth fear the LORD; let all the people of the world revere him' (verse 8).

Even non-Christian writers are moved to express their wonder at the complexity and splendour of the universe. As theologian Don Carson once said, 'It takes an enormous act of the will on the part of even the most cynical of scientists instead to look at it all and say, "Ah, it's just physics. Stop admiring it. Don't do that. There's no design. It's just molecules bumping into molecules." '[6]

God's creation speaks of God's majesty. As Psalm 19 proclaims, 'The heavens declare the glory of God; the skies proclaim the work of his hands.' John Goldingay reminds us that, since creation expresses God's glory and his steadfast love, it is an embodiment of God's commitment to us.[7]

Not only does God speak a powerful word, but he speaks a reliable word.

A reliable word

'He commanded, and it stood firm' (verse 9).

There is a stability and reliability to the world which God has made. We've already seen in verse 4 that his word is dependable. And there is a connection between God's character and his word – his word is right and true because *he* is reliable, and he creates that which is reliable.

Other psalms, like 119, affirm the same thing. You can stake your life on the truth of God's word. It's because God is eternal. He is the one true, living God who fills the entire universe, and so obviously his word is the same. 'Your word, LORD, is eternal; it stands firm in the heavens' (Psalm 119:89). And it makes the same connection that we have already seen in Psalm 33. 'You are righteous, LORD, and your laws are right' (Psalm 119:137). So when we say God's word is true, we mean it exactly corresponds to reality. It is completely reliable. As Eugene Peterson expresses it, 'For Yahweh's word is solid to the core.'[8]

This means that the created world – the entire universe – has a stability, a predictability, which allows scientists to refer to 'natural laws'. Indeed, this is one of the main assumptions on which scientific enterprise is built. We discover an intelligible and delicately balanced structure. There is a reliability about natural laws – a reliability about the operations of the universe – because of the reliability of the God who spoke the world into being: 'He commanded, and it stood firm' (verse 9).

So what is reality? It is founded on the *God who is*, and the *God who speaks* a powerful and a reliable word. He is the central reference point for everything in our lives and in this universe.

Have you noticed that in verse 6 the psalmist speaks of God's word and God's breath? Michael Wilcock says that the New Testament will give capitals to the Word (verses 4, 6, 9) and the Breath (verse 6), for they tell us of the Son and the Spirit, one with the Father from all eternity. John doubtless had this psalm in mind when we wrote his Gospel: 'In the beginning was the Word, and the Word was with God, and the Word was God . . . Through him all things were made; without him nothing was made that has been made' (John 1:1–3).

Psalm 104 is another profound psalm that describes the nature of reality, and in verse 24 we read: 'How many are your works, LORD! In wisdom you made them all.' The Jews wrote about the divine intelligence or 'wisdom' that informed the creation process. When Paul wrote about Christ in Colossians 1, he used some Old Testament Jewish background, but he explains that, central to the creation – to its design and purpose – lies not a divine attribute, but a divine person. Jesus was the agent of creation: 'in him all things were created' (verse 16). And he is the purpose of creation: 'all things have been created . . . for him' (verse 16). That points to the key issue which science cannot address. Paul shows us that Jesus is the key to understanding the 'why' of the universe and the 'why' of our lives. We are made *by* him and we are made *for* him. And then Paul goes further: 'In him all things hold together' (verse 17). We should link this with Colossians 2:3: '[In Christ] are hidden all the treasures of wisdom and knowledge.' All of our knowledge comes into focus around this reality – Jesus Christ who is the Truth. Truth is a coherent whole because of the common focus that ties it together.

Maybe you've had the experience of wearing 3D glasses. You need them to watch a 3D movie, but my first opportunity to use them was when they came as a free gift with a packet of breakfast cereal – you had to wear the glasses to see the 3D picture on the back of the packet.

It was a chaotic picture, until you put on the glasses, and there it was – a wonderful work of art in glorious Technicolour. As we mentioned earlier, 'in your light', in the Light of Christ, 'we see light'. The Christian worldview focuses on Christ, the living Word. Do you remember how Paul expressed it in 2 Corinthians 4:6? 'For God, who said, "Let light shine out of darkness," made his light shine in our hearts to give us the light of the knowledge of God's glory displayed in the face of Christ.'

The foundations of reality are, first, related to *the reality of the God who is*; second, to *the reality of the God who speaks*. And in the next section of the psalm we come to a third theme.

3. The reality of the God who rules (verses 10–19)

The writer now describes how God is not only the Creator, but he is also the King. We can summarize this section by looking at his *purposeful* rule and his *compassionate* rule.

A *purposeful rule*

> The LORD foils the plans of the nations;
>> he thwarts the purposes of the peoples.
> But the plans of the LORD stand firm for ever,
>> the purposes of his heart through all generations
> (verses 10–11)

Here is one of Richard Dawkins's oft-quoted statements:

> In a universe of blind physical forces and genetic
> replication, some people are going to get hurt, other
> people are going to get lucky, and you won't find any
> rhyme or reason in it, nor any justice. The universe we
> observe has precisely the properties we should expect if
> there is, at bottom, no design, no purpose, no evil, and
> no good, nothing but blind, pitiless indifference . . .
> DNA neither knows nor cares. DNA just is. And we
> dance to its music.[9]

When I was a student back in the 1970s, this used to be called 'nothing-buttery'. It's a way of reducing everything to physics – nothing but blind forces, nothing but DNA. But it clearly fails to tell the whole story. Psalm 33 tells us that *God is*, that *God speaks* this universe into being, and that *God has purposes and plans* for his creation, for his universe, and even for you and me. It follows that if he is the eternal God, the God who brought everything into being, who sustains everything by the word of his power, then he is sovereign – he rules. Creation and history are both under the direction of the same God.

That's why, as verse 10 highlights, God cancels the schemes of empires, why he opposes human pride and unbelief: 'The LORD foils the plans of the nations; he thwarts the purposes of the peoples.' In the Old Testament 'the nations' often referred to the hostile superpowers like Assyria or Babylon or Persia. It would have seemed to

God's people as though the foreign policies of these super-powers were the decisive factor in the world. But Psalm 33 says it is Yahweh's policy, it is his will and purpose; that is the decisive factor. God isn't intimidated by the power of nations. God's people were mistaken if they thought that the decisions made in Babylon were more important than those made in heaven. God's people needed a change of perspective. And it's the same for us. The centre of power today is not Washington, or Moscow, or Iran, or Islamic State – it is the Lord God omnipotent.

His eternal purposes, shaped by his steadfast love, will stand firm: 'The plans of the LORD stand firm for ever, the purposes of his heart through all generations' (verse 11). Everything is under his control. As Psalm 115:3 expresses it: 'Our God is in heaven; he does whatever pleases him.' But this is not simply a remote bureaucracy. The atheist Christopher Hitchens was wrong when he argued that the idea of 'a creator and a plan meant a celestial dictatorship is installed to supervise us, a kind of divine North Korea'.[10] The sovereignty of God interacts with the responsibility of his people as they grasp opportunities, make decisions, give themselves wholeheartedly to a particular course of action. He is the personal God, and he has good purposes for you and me. We repeat once again: 'The earth is full of his unfailing love.'

We could turn to Psalm 139 to remind ourselves that his creative work includes each one of us: 'You knit me together in my mother's womb' (Psalm 139:13). Or express it in Pauline language: 'We are God's handiwork, created in Christ Jesus to do good works, which God prepared in advance for us to do' (Ephesians 2:10). Peter Lewis once said that it's not enough to know the genetic map of the individual. We also need to have a map of how and why we are to live. That's why we need to understand the psalm – the reality of God's purposeful rule.

Further, his purposeful rule included his choice of the nation of Israel. Look at verse 12: 'Blessed is the nation whose God is the LORD, the people he chose for his inheritance.' His purpose in choosing Israel was for a unique destiny, that through them all the families of the earth would be blessed. This too is an expression of his steadfast love which fills the earth. Through his will and purpose, through his election of Israel, through the mission of his Son, his good purposes for all people are being fulfilled.

A compassionate rule

> From heaven the LORD looks down
>> and sees all mankind;
> from his dwelling-place he watches
>> all who live on earth –
> he who forms the hearts of all,
>> who considers everything they do.
> (verses 13–15)

The psalmist is reminding us that God literally oversees his world. Every human life is known to him, and every human life is accountable to him. The fact is, God is no absentee landlord. Psalm 104 underlines it time and again:

> He waters the mountains . . .
> He makes grass grow . . .
> When you open your hand
>   they are satisfied . . .
> When you take away their breath,
>   they die and return to the dust.
> (verses 13–14, 28–29)

He knows and cares about his creation. To quote Colossians 1 once again, Jesus Christ is the Sustainer of creation: 'in him all things hold together' (verse 17).

I have often travelled on a section of the M5 which was carefully constructed on stilts, to climb the hills near Gordano, south of Bristol. It is a very fine piece of engineering, and I read some while ago that the engineer responsible decided to build a house in the hills adjacent to that stretch of motorway. And as I have driven that section, I have often imagined him at home with a glass of sherry in his hand, his feet up, admiring his handiwork. Some people imagine God is like that, but it is a distorted picture. Having brought this world into being, he isn't sitting in his celestial armchair, passive towards the universe he has made. He is always active, engaged in caring for the world day by day. The writer to the Hebrews says the same as he introduces Jesus: 'He upholds the universe by the word of his power'[11] (Hebrews 1:3). This is another aspect of reality. Here is John Owen's comment on this verse:

> Such is the nature and condition of the universe, that it could not subsist for a moment, nor could anything in it act regularly unto its appointed end, without the continued support, guidance, influence, disposal of the Son of God.

He goes on to point out how foolish it is to oppose God's purposes. As he puts it, 'Their very lives are at the disposal of Him whom they oppose.'[12]

Psalm 33 makes the point in verses 16 and 17. If God is the ruler of all, then there is no point in trying to place your trust elsewhere: '

> No king is saved by the size of his army;
>   no warrior escapes by his great strength.
> A horse is a vain hope for deliverance;
>   despite all its great strength it cannot save.

Finally, the idea of the God who sees is also picked up in verse 18, but now in a more personal way:

> But the eyes of the LORD are on those who fear him,
>   on those whose hope is in his unfailing love,
> to deliver them from death
>   and keep them alive in famine.
> (verses 18, 19)

I remember my mother used to say to me, 'I've got my eye on you!' That usually meant, 'Stop larking around.' It was the same with my teachers, who had 'eyes in the back of their heads'. 'I can see you, Lamb; don't try anything.' But verse 18 is different. His eyes are on 'those whose hope is in his unfailing love'. It describes God's loving oversight, his protective care, his sheltering us from evil. He is the Sovereign Lord, yet he is also the Father who cares, who fulfils his gracious purposes, as verses 18 and 19 declare – the God who protects, feeds, delivers and rescues. He truly is the God of salvation.

As the psalm began with *a call to rejoice*, it now ends with a *call to hope* (verses 20–22). How do we respond to these three great realities: *the God who is, the God who speaks, the God who rules*? The psalm concludes by encouraging us to fear him (verse 18), to hope in him (verse 18), to wait for him (verse 20), to trust in him (verse 21), and again, to hope in him (verse 22). The Lord is calling us to believe that the created universe, and history, and humankind, and the future – all are in his hands. And as we have seen, all of this is ultimately fulfilled in Jesus Christ, who is the Saviour who reveals God's steadfast love, the Word who brought all things into being, the King who rules, and in whom, one day, everything will find its completion. To put our hope in him is to align ourselves with his rule in this world. It is to go with the grain of how this world is made. Psalm 33 is a song that transforms our perspective on life, the universe and everything. It is a psalm with a profound vision of reality. It is a call to trust this God with everything we have, knowing that we are roped to the safest guide in the universe.

I often quote the words of William McConnell, Deputy Governor of the Maze Prison in Northern Ireland, shortly before he was assassinated:

> I have committed my life, my talents, work and
> action to Almighty God, in the sure and certain
> knowledge that, however slight my hold on him
> may have been . . . his promises are sure and his hold
> on me complete.

Let's join with all of God's people through the centuries in praying the final verse of the psalm:

> May your unfailing love be with us, LORD,
>   even as we put our hope in you.

Notes

1. C. S. Lewis, *Essay Collection: Faith, Christianity and the Church* (HarperCollins, 2002), p. 21.
2. Michael Wilcock, *The Message of Psalms 1–72*, The Bible Speaks Today series (IVP, 2001), p. 113.
3. Madeleine Bunting, 'No wonder atheists are angry: they seem ready to believe anything', *The Guardian*, http://www.guardian.co.uk/media/2006/jan/07/raceandreligion.comment (31 July 2008).
4. Michael Wilcock, *The Message of Psalms 1–72*, p. 112.

5. Derek Kidner, *Psalms 1–72*, Tyndale Old Testament Commentary (IVP, 1973), p. 136.

6. Don Carson, *The God Who Is There: Finding Your Place in God's Story* (Baker Books, 2010), p. 17.

7. John Goldingay, *Psalms, Volume 1* (Baker Academic, 2006), p. 468.

8. Psalm 33:4, *The Message*.

9. Richard Dawkins, *River out of Eden: A Darwinian View of Life* (Basic Books, 1995), p. 133.

10. Live debate with Tony Blair, November 2010.

11. ESV.

12. John Owen, quoted in Andrew Wilson, *Incomparable* (David C. Cook, 2007), p. 41.

The Lord of the Kings

by Chris Sinkinson

Chris Sinkinson has been involved in local church-based ministry in Canterbury and Bournemouth. He is now pastor of Alderholt Chapel near Salisbury. Having studied theology at Bristol University, he is part of the teaching team at Moorlands College on the south coast. His interests in the background to Bible history have motivated him to lead a number of tours to Israel and be part of an archaeological dig in Galilee. Chris has published a book on apologetics, *Confident Christianity*, and a guide to the Old Testament, *Time Travel to the Old Testament* (both IVP), and *Backchat: Answering Christianity's Critics* (Christian Focus). Married to Ros, he has two lively and energetic boys, Thomas and Toby, who love rambling in the great outdoors.

The Lord of the Kings: 1 Kings 8:6–21

It was said of Gilly Cooper, who went to Godolphin School, Salisbury, not far from where I now live: 'Gilly has set herself an extremely low standard which she has failed to maintain.' John Lennon, Quarry Park School, Liverpool: 'Certainly on the road to failure, hopeless, rather a clown in class, wasting other people's time.' Eric Morecambe, Lancaster Road Junior School: 'I hate to say this but Eric will never get anywhere in life.' Norman Wisdom, though this was not actually a school report, but his army education centre report: 'The boy is every inch a fool, but luckily for him he is not very tall.'

Don't judge anyone too soon. Don't judge the story too soon. Sometimes we mistake our journey for our destination. Sometimes we write people off, and yet they are on a journey; they are not at their destination.

I mentioned yesterday that in this Bible expedition we might have thought that after the exodus we had reached our destination. God had called a people to himself, the Israelites, rescued them from slavery, given them a land. Job done. Journey over. It might look that way in the passage before us this morning. We come now to Israel's golden age, and yet we are going to see it is an age of disappointment. We are not there yet.

An age of construction

My first heading: this is an 'age of construction', particularly in verses 6–13. You see, on our expedition we have reached some high hills this morning. From the valley of slavery in Egypt, over the Great Sea, the Israelites have come to settle in this small plot of land called Canaan, and despite tribal differences there is essentially a family unity among them. Under the first kings they form a united kingdom of Israel. The reading we had details the time of King Solomon, his building work and particularly the building of the temple. This is the golden age of the Old Testament. Under King David and King Solomon there is a time of unity, prosperity and relative peace for the nation that they will never see again. For that reason, some critics dismiss this as a legendary age. King David is relegated to a kind of King Arthur figure of the ancient world; King Solomon, merely a matter of myth. But such dismissals play fast and loose with the evidence.

Recent evidence brings back onto the pages of history the reality of David and Solomon. I want to share some of that with you now. Excavations in Jerusalem have revealed the city of King David, with remains of houses and extensive structures that fit this time and place. There is an impressive stone structure which is now generally believed to have been part of the supporting foundations for a great palace at the time of David and Solomon.

Events from so long ago are hard to find direct evidence for. As the centuries pass, documents tend to disappear, disintegrate. Architecture is the most that we can hope for. Even King Herod from the time of Jesus, a thousand years after David, is only really known from his building work, his architecture. If you visit the Holy Land, most of the impressive sites you see are the buildings from the time of King Herod, a remarkable planner and architect. In fact, apart from coins bearing his name, we have no inscriptions of King Herod's name from his time. But no-one doubts the existence of King Herod; his building work was so significant.

But King David and Solomon have regularly been dismissed as figures of legend or myth. Yet that claim was blown away in the early 1990s by an astonishing discovery of a commemorative stone. This was found at Dan, a city in the north of Israel, dating to within a hundred years of the life of King David. It refers to the house of King David, to his dynasty as well as the house of Israel. This broken stone, nearly 3,000 years old, in Aramaic script, is a direct reference to the historical figure and dynasty of

King David. No longer could he be dismissed as a King Arthur-like figure of mythology; King David is back in the history books.

What about King Solomon? What evidence do we have of his reign? Well, something very interesting emerged during the 1960s, in the early period of archaeological excavation in Israel. From the 1960s onwards, at three cities, a certain type of fortified gateway emerged. It's called the six-chambered gate, a very secure system for preserving and guarding a city wall. And at Hazor, Megiddo and Gezer, three cities that are mentioned by name in the Bible as having been fortified by Solomon, we find the same architecture, the same style of six-chambered fortified gate. All of this indicates that at this period of history, the time of King Solomon, there was wealth, there was central planning and there was a great mind coming up with a great new architectural idea. These have the fingerprints of King Solomon all over them. They provide a record of the existence of Solomon and that golden age of Israel's history.

Of course, most famously in terms of building work is the great temple. Since the exodus, when the Israelites came out of Egypt, they stored the ark of the covenant with the stone tablets of the law in a portable tent, the tabernacle. Solomon created a permanent stone version of the tabernacle – we call it the temple.

The priests then brought the ark of the LORD's covenant to its place in the inner sanctuary of the temple, the

Most Holy Place, and put it beneath the wings of the cherubim.

(Verse 6)

It is interesting that the basic outline, shape or structure of the temple with the tabernacle was not unique to ancient Israel. An outer courtyard, an inner holy place, a small Holy of Holies at the very back, all oriented eastwards – you find that structure outside of Israel. What was unique was not the structure of the temple nor its shape; what was unique was what lay at its heart. Instead of housing a throne for a king or a statue to a national god, there were words. The Word of God. The law of God. That was the physical object placed in the Holy of Holies. As if to say, it's not going to be a physical statue of God that you will worship; you will worship God through his Word. He will speak and you will hear. That is why Christians and Jews down through the years have been known as a 'people of the Book'. At the heart of Christian worship is a God who speaks, a God whom we know through his spoken Word. So God makes himself known through his Word, and yet, the Israelites have a visible, tangible sense of his presence. Look at verses 10–11:

When the priests withdrew from the Holy Place, the cloud filled the temple of the LORD. And the priests could not perform their service because of the cloud, for the glory of the LORD filled the temple.

God gave a physical sense of his presence in the temple. Where have we seen that cloud before? The cloud of God's presence is a reminder of the pillar of cloud we saw yesterday in the exodus. The pillar of cloud was the representation of God's visible, felt presence among the people of God, and now here it is filling the temple. It is what the Bible calls the 'glory of God'. That word 'glory' seems such a vague word; it passes over our heads. But the Hebrew word 'glory' has a sense of meaning 'heaviness' or 'weight'. The glory of God is the heavy, weighty, felt presence of God among the people, and here he is in the temple. So this age of construction is a great glory to this age. God is present among the people.

The age of contentment

That leads me to a second heading: this is an 'age of contentment'. When critics ask for evidence of this period, it is worth noticing how short-lived it really is. Solomon's reign, the high point of ancient Israel, lasts for about forty years. Even during that time, we read that Egypt launches a military campaign into the land. So it is forty years not without some trouble. In other words, let's not misread this golden age to imagine that Israel has no problems or enemies, or that it lasts for hundreds of years. It is a brief moment. It quickly passes in biblical history. An age of contentment that is gone in a blink of an eye in terms of world history, and I think there is an important reason for that which we will return to in a moment.

The evidence that people would really like to see for this age is the evidence for the temple at the time of King Solomon. Surely, of all the buildings of the Bible this is the one we should have the clearest evidence for. But there's a problem primarily because the temple built by Solomon was demolished, rebuilt a few hundred years later, extensively remodelled by King Herod at the time of Jesus, demolished by the Romans who then built their own mini-temple that was then demolished, and when Islam arrived, they built their own commemorative monument. That makes archaeology very difficult there. So at this Muslim holy site, probably the most hotly contested piece of real estate in the entire world, little archeological work goes on.

The golden Dome of the Rock, which we still see in our evening news so often, is an Islamic holy site, built at the time of Mohammed over the location where the temple would have stood for 1,400 years, preventing any kind of significant exploration into the earlier periods that would lie beneath.

One summer actually, a few years ago, Moorlands Bible College students were able to come with me, and we took part in a very tantalizing dig, what's called the 'Temple Mount Sifting Project'. The authorities who control this area control that golden dome and in their wisdom they decided to do some extensive reworking. They brought in some earth movers, dug out some ground, laid some pipe, upgraded the electrics and dumped all of the excavated soil, debris and rock into the

Kidron Valley nearby. So an archaeological team have been sifting through the debris, wet-sifting it, to discover every little fragment of stone, marble, tile, coin or weapon. Taking part in the dig was so intriguing. The objects that emerged show that there was something significant there, but of course they were all muddled up and out of context, and it is hard to understand how they relate to the various areas of occupation.

So we might just want to give up, believing we will never know about the location of the temple at the time of Solomon. Except that something recently emerged that is a very interesting indicator of where the temple stood, and evidence for the time of Solomon. Inside the golden dome is a discovery that has literally been on display these past 2,000 years, but no-one noticed it. If you were to look down on an aerial view from inside the golden dome, you would see the rocky outcrop. When King Herod remodelled the Temple Mount, it looked like a flat platform, but inside that golden dome there is preserved a rocky outcrop that would have been the peak of Mount Moriah. This would have been the location where Abraham would have taken Isaac, and this is the location where the Holy of Holies would have stood. This golden dome has preserved, in effect, that rocky outcrop, the remains of that peak of Mount Moriah.

Dutch archaeologist Leen Ritmeyer has carried out some of the most extensive surveys of the entire area of the Temple Mount, quite literally inch by inch. Looking at photographs of this rocky outcrop, he saw a rectangular cut-out in the rock. He measured it, and this rectangular cut-out fits perfectly the dimensions of the ark of the covenant, the exact centre of the Holy of Holies. It is a footprint of where the ark of the covenant stood at the time of King Solomon. Preserved by that golden dome is our fingerprint of the time of King Solomon when the ark of the covenant stood in the temple.

Verse 15: 'Praise be to the LORD, the God of Israel, who with his own hand has fulfilled what he promised with his own mouth to my father David.' You see, these are physical representations of God's faithfulness to his Word. God had promised the temple; God fulfilled his promise. God promised to live among his people; God fulfilled his promise. God is true to his promises. God said in creation, 'Let there be light', and there was light. God said the Egyptians would be destroyed in the Great Sea, and they were destroyed. God said that Israel would have a land and that God would dwell among them, and they had a land and a temple. So this section of Bible history, this age of contentment, at one level is about the fulfilment of God's promises.

1 Kings chapter 4, verse 25:

During Solomon's lifetime Judah and Israel, from Dan to Beersheba, lived in safety, everyone under their own vine and under their own fig-tree.

God now has a people of his own, in a land they can call their own. With prosperity, with relative security, they are under God's rule; they know his presence. As God walked in the garden of Eden with Adam and Eve in the cool of the day, now God in the cloud of his glory lives in the temple in the midst of his people. So no wonder Solomon can use these words in his prayer in 1 Kings 8 verse 20:

> The LORD has kept the promise he made: I have succeeded David my father and now I sit on the throne of Israel, just as the LORD promised, and I have built the temple for the Name of the LORD, the God of Israel.

It sounds to me like the Bible could or should stop there. This is the place where people can have their sin forgiven, they can know a right relationship with God, they have the temple, they know that their sacrifices can be offered, their sins can be covered, they can come before a holy God. Surely this is where the Bible could stop? We have reached the golden age. This is where we should be living. But something is not right. And that is why my final heading this morning is 'The age of compromise'.

The age of compromise

I hope you have time to get out walking. If you do, I hope you take the right precautions, wear the right raincoat and the right boots for your terrain. But happily, one precaution we don't need to take out here in the Lake District, that you would if you were in Canada, is looking out for bears. My wife and I were in Canada in the Rocky Mountains many years ago now, and the Canadian park authorities produce a little guide to help walkers tell the difference between brown bears and black bears. Apparently getting this right can be a matter of life and death, because the evasive action you need to take depends on which kind of bear you encounter. So this is free – I'm going to give you this advice now – if you are attacked by a brown bear, the best thing to do is play dead and it will ignore you. However, if you play dead with a black bear, it will eat you. A good idea might be to try to climb a tree. If it is a brown bear, it will not follow. However, if it is a black bear, it will follow you up the tree. How do you tell the difference between a brown bear and a black bear? Unfortunately, it is not the colour of their fur, because the guide helpfully points out that often a black bear will be brown in colour. The guide says the best way of telling them apart is by their droppings. Which of course raises the question: wouldn't it be too late by then?

You see, superficial judgments are dangerous. What on the outside appearance may look OK or acceptable, underneath may be quite different. What is going on in this golden age for Israel? Are things all that they appear to be? Notice in verse 27 in Solomon's prayer that he asks a question: 'But will God really dwell on earth? The heavens, even the highest heaven, cannot contain you. How much less this temple I have built!' Now you see, it is Solomon's turn to ask the *Really?* question that we have been asking this week.

Can God really dwell on earth? It is a good question to ask. We know that God demonstrated his presence in the temple, a cloud of his presence, a felt sense of the glory of God. But he didn't literally live there. God fills all of space; he cannot literally be limited by a temple. But I think there is more behind the question than that. This is not simply a question of physical space – you see there is a lot going on in this golden age that I haven't told you about. I haven't told you that Solomon marries many wives and keeps many mistresses. I haven't told you that many of those mistresses led him to worship other gods. I haven't told you that the nation, after his death, will break in two and that the Northern Kingdom will set up all sorts of false places of worship. I haven't told you that that Northern Kingdom will eventually be destroyed and wiped off the map, that the small Southern Kingdom will form alliances with pagan nations that will lead them astray, that the ark of the covenant will literally vanish altogether, that the remaining people, nicknamed 'Jews' – it is just short for Judea, their tribe – those remaining people will be taken away into captivity.

Three hundred years after Solomon, a prophet, a visionary in Israel, will see something very dramatic take place. In Ezekiel 10:18 he will say, 'Then the glory of the LORD departed from over the threshold of the temple.' Now it is true that a remnant will return, a smaller temple will be rebuilt, but it is nothing compared to the temple of Solomon, and the Jews will never again become, in the ancient world, an independent nation. In the ancient world they will be ruled by the Persians, by the Greeks, by the Romans.

'Can God really dwell in a temple?' asks Solomon. No, not really. You see, if there is something this golden age of Solomon clearly reveals, it is that we've got a problem, not solved even by the temple of stone. You see what is our greatest need? Freedom from slavery. The Israelites got that in the exodus, but they remain enslaved to their passions. A land of your own? The Israelites got that, and look at it today. What about the needs that Solomon had met? Material wealth, wisdom, song-writing ability, buildings – Solomon had all of these. Solomon had many wives and mistresses. Do you think that your greatest need this morning is for a boyfriend or a girlfriend or a partner? Do you think this morning that your greatest need is for a religion? For a temple of stone? Do you think your greatest need is for your career to be furthered? To get the money to feel comfortable with? Look back in history: we have reached mountains in ancient Israel's history, the golden age of Solomon, but we've climbed a false summit.

If you are on a quest for true happiness, you need to set your sights higher. You see, wealth without Jesus Christ, a partner without Jesus Christ, land without Jesus Christ, none of these answers our deepest need; none of them addresses the problem of our broken relationship with God. Without Christ, they do not satisfy. Without Christ, they don't bring inner transformation. Without Christ, they don't bring complete forgiveness. Solomon proved it. Jesus said these words in Matthew 6:28–29, 32–33:

Why do you worry about clothes? See how the flowers of the field grow. They do not labour or spin. Yet I tell you that not even Solomon in all his splendour was dressed like one of these . . . Your heavenly Father knows that you need them. But seek first his kingdom and his righteousness, and all these things will be given to you as well.

Don't seek money as the most important thing in your life. Don't make finding a partner your top priority. Don't seek religion as if it will address your deepest need. Don't seek temples or achievements or careers or success as your number-one concern. Seek Christ. Seek first the kingdom of God, that right relationship with God where our sin is forgiven. Seek what was lost in Genesis chapter 3: it is where you belong. You belong in that right relationship with God, and without Christ, all those other things are as nothing. But with Christ, we have it all. So from this false summit we can glimpse the real peak. The real peak is another mountain top, not capped by a temple of stone, but capped by a cross. And that is where our expedition is going to take us tomorrow. From a false summit to the true summit. From a temple of stone to a temple who is Jesus Christ.

What Hope Is There?

by Vaughan Roberts

Vaughan came to faith as he read through Matthew's Gospel for himself as a teenager. After studying law at Cambridge University and a brief spell doing student ministry in South Africa, he moved to Oxford to study theology at Wycliffe Hall, and has lived in the city ever since. In 1991 he joined the staff of St Ebbe's Church to lead the student ministry, and since 1998 he has been Rector. He is also the Director of the Proclamation Trust, an organization that encourages and equips Bible teachers. In his spare time Vaughan writes books and plays tennis and golf.

What Hope Is There? Romans 8:18–38

Well, what a great few days we've had. I love Keswick, it's a huge joy for me to be here, and I really enjoy not just preaching God's Word – that's certainly a huge privilege – but hearing God's Word as well. Tomorrow I will head home. On my way home I will go to the British Open – not playing golf by the way, in case there is any confusion, just watching! Then back to normal pretty soon. And how easy it is when we go back to normal to forget all the good things that we have heard.

What are you taking back with you?

At the end of a busy week, where we have heard an awful lot of things, can I encourage you to think: what is the big thing that I must not forget as I head home? Maybe a truth that I knew before but really need to internalize and delight in again. Maybe a specific challenge, something in my life that needs to change. Tell someone – husband, wife, family member, friend. Pray about it and ask God to help you to change in the light of what we've heard.

Paul did not write the letter of Romans so that people could study it in theological colleges and pass exams. He wrote it for a very practical purpose. He wrote it to expound the gospel to a church he had never been to, that they might recognize errors that people make about it, understand it deeply, take it in, and then live it out in the way they relate to one another as a united church and in every area of life. Live it out and get it out – this is the gospel for the world. It's the only gospel for the world, and the world desperately needs to hear it.

Throughout the week we've been looking at various questions the world asks that the gospel answers. And today's question is: 'What hope is there?' That is a massively important question because many people live without hope. We live in a world that, in the West at least, is increasingly turning its back on God. And once you've turned your back on God, you have no fundamental meaning to life, you've got no purpose, you've got nothing beyond the grave, death is the end. So it is no wonder that people live for the moment if there is no future. This is the age of the instant: instant coffee, instant credit, instant returns. It's summed up for me by an old credit-card advert a number of years ago. Do you remember Access? The advert said, 'Access takes the waiting out of wanting.' So we want to live for now; we don't want to wait for anything. But it's no wonder that with that kind of attitude there is a disconnect with the Christian faith. We find it hard to engage with a Christian faith which speaks so much about the future.

We saw this yesterday in Romans 8:17: 'Now if we are children, then we are heirs – heirs of God and co-heirs with Christ, if indeed we share in his sufferings in order that we may also share in his glory.' Most of the blessings of the Christian life lie in the future. In the meantime we can expect suffering. It is so vital for us, if we are going to survive as Christians, that we have right expectations of what the Christian life will be like. Imagine, if you will, a Bible line of expectation. Here's what the Bible said we should be expecting in the Christian life, and we must not live below the line. Many of us do that all the time. We don't live in the light of all God has given to us in Christ. We live in accordance with the 'kidney-donor view' of the Christian life which says, 'I've got a certificate of justification in my purse, in my wallet; it's useless in this life, but it will be useful in the next life. I've got a statement that I'm in the right with God, but it doesn't change anything now.' Paul says, 'No! You've not just got a new status, but a new life. You can change; the Spirit transforms you.' Don't live below the line.

But by the same token, don't live above the line. Don't claim for now, what has only been promised then. Don't expect sinlessness in this life. Don't expect a life free of suffering. Note Paul says in verse 17 that glory is still to come. In the meantime, expect to suffer. But far from leading to despair, that suffering is the road we must travel on the way to glory. The destination is not in doubt.

In this final section of Romans 8 there are two main themes: suffering and certainty. Both appear in both sections of our passage, but the first section we might say majors more on suffering, and the theme of certainty comes even more powerfully in the second section.

The suffering of the Christian

Let's begin with the suffering of the Christian (verses 18–27). Dominated by this theme of groaning, this passage has been described as 'a symphony of sighing'. We have got the groans of creation in verse 22, the groans of the Christian in verse 23 and the groans of the Spirit in verse 26.

The groans of creation

Verse 18: 'I consider that our present sufferings are not worth comparing with the glory that will be revealed in us.' Now don't misunderstand that. He is not for a moment belittling the suffering that we might experience in this life. Some of you, I know, have experienced terrible suffering and right now are going through terrible suffering. Maybe the private agony of depression? You feel as if no-one really understands. Or the almost physical pain of bereavement? It is as if you have lost a limb. Or the anguish of shattered hopes? The relationship that seemed so promising suddenly comes to an end. Or maybe the sense of exclusion because of your faith? Paul is not saying these are nothing; he is simply saying, however great they are, and they may be very great, they are nothing *compared* to the wonder of the glory that is to come. He is not belittling the suffering, just magnifying what is to come.

What is your view on glory or the future? Some people have the impression that heaven is basically an immaterial world where souls float around in nothingness – the only substantial thing is an occasional harp. It's not very exciting, is it? The Bible says, 'No! If you're not excited about the future, you haven't even begun to understand how amazing it is. It's so great, that the whole of creation is longing for it.' Verse 19 begins with the word 'for': 'For the creation waits in eager expectation for the children of God to be revealed.' Paul is saying, 'Let me tell you how amazing your glory will be. The whole of creation is, as it were, on tiptoes longing for it – for the moment when the sons and daughters, the children of God, will be revealed.'

At the moment we are not revealed. We don't have a Ready Brek glow around us that marks us out as children of glory. If you look around people in your town, Christians look much the same as everybody else. We get sick, we suffer, we die. A Christian in hospital or in the morgue looks exactly like a non-Christian. We have not yet been revealed. But the moment will come when the children of God are revealed. The glory of God will be revealed in us. We will be restored fully into the image of God, we will reflect his glory perfectly, and creation cannot wait for that day because it is an important moment for the whole of creation as well.

Verses 20–21:

> For the creation was subjected to frustration, not by its
> own choice, but by the will of the one who subjected it,
> in hope that the creation itself will be liberated from its
> bondage to decay and brought into the freedom and glory
> of the children of God.

We were made by God to rule over creation. When we
turned away from God, that had terrible implications, not
just for us, but for the whole created order. Creation is, as it
were, put out of joint. It's subjected to frustration, bondage
and decay. That never-ending cycle of life followed by death
– a flower appears and then withers, a leaf buds and then
falls – continues year after year, century after century, life
being forever snuffed out by death. But actually not forever,
because as creation shared in our curse, so it will share in
our salvation, which is why it is longing for our final redemption. Meanwhile, it's crying out in frustration and groaning.

Verse 22: 'We know that the whole creation has been
groaning as in the pains of childbirth right up to the present
time.' If we only have ears to hear it, we can hear creation
groaning in the rumblings of an earthquake or a volcano,
in the raging of the sea. The green lobby is absolutely right
to care about this world. God made it. He loves it. Christians
should be very concerned about the environment. But
those in the green lobby who despair about the world are
wrong. The groans of creation are not the death pangs
of the natural world; they are cries of pain much more

positive than that. Like the pangs of childbirth, they are very painful, but productive. It's leading to glory; the end is not in doubt. Creation will be perfected.

Do not think that the final destination is for us to go to heaven when we die, and float around in nothingness. Remember where the Bible began. God made the heavens and the earth. Matter matters, because God made it. And when human beings turned away from God, that didn't just affect our souls; it affected our bodies; it affected the whole natural world. And God is a big God, and salvation is massive. It's not just about our souls; it's going to affect our bodies, it's going to affect the whole created order. Yes, we are with God in heaven when we die, absolutely safe and secure, but the ultimate goal is a new creation. A new heaven, a new earth. Do you remember John in Revelation 21:1–2 said, 'Then I saw, "a new heaven and a new earth" . . . coming down out of heaven from God.' C. S. Lewis, as so often, gets it just right in one of the Narnia books:

> 'Those hills,' said Lucy, 'the nice woody ones and the blue ones behind – aren't they very like the Southern border of Narnia?' 'Like!' cried Edmund after a moment's silence. 'Why, they are exactly like. Look there's Mount Pire with his forked head, and there's the pass into Archenland and everything!' 'And yet they're not like,' said Lucy. 'They're different. They have more colours on them and they look further away than I remembered and they're more . . . more . . . oh, I don't know . . .' 'More like the real thing,' said the Lord Digory softly.[1]

This world is the shadow lands. The world to come is the substance. The new creation.

The groans of the Christian

Then there are the groans of creation, groans too of the Christian (verses 23–25). We groan as well: 'Not only so, but we ourselves, who have the firstfruits of the Spirit, groan inwardly as we wait eagerly for our adoption to sonship, the redemption of our bodies' (verse 23). Yes, we receive the Spirit and that's wonderful – don't live below the line – but we have just received the firstfruits of the Spirit. The firstfruits are the first signs that the full harvest is coming. The odd grain of wheat here, the odd grain of wheat there, are a sign of things to come. We've received the firstfruits of the Spirit; we do not have full salvation now. We are still waiting for the redemption of our bodies. That hasn't happened yet. And so do not expect full healing now. God can heal – of course he can, he is a sovereign God – but he hasn't promised to. One day our bodies will be redeemed. We will be perfectly restored. Meanwhile, we groan. We've had the firstfruits, we've had a taste of glory, we've had a taste of what we are going to enjoy fully in the world to come, and once you've got a taste of something, you want it more, don't you?

It's terrible when someone's cooking in the kitchen and you long for a taste. You have a taste, and if you hadn't had that taste, it wouldn't have been too bad waiting until later, but having had the taste, you want more. And we've had a taste, a taste of what it means to hate sin and to love holiness. We want more. We want to be perfectly holy. We've got a taste for what it means to be loved by God and to know God intimately, but we don't see him yet and we long for more. That frustration, that longing, is a really good sign. It's a sign that the Holy Spirit is in us – he's given us a taste, the firstfruits; we want more, we are groaning.

The groans of the Spirit

Then there are the groans of the Spirit (verses 26–27). We are weak, and sometimes we feel our weakness very, very deeply because of our sin and the suffering we have to endure. Sometimes it's almost more than we can bear and we don't know how or even what to pray. The best we can do is groan. The groan speaks of our frustration of ourselves, of the world, and our longing for the world to come. It's as if we are just saying, 'Urghhh!' – we can't put it into words and we are not alone. Paul says the Holy Spirit groans with us: 'In the same way, the Spirit helps us in our weakness. We do not know what we ought to pray for, but the Spirit himself intercedes for us through wordless groans' (verse 26). Even within the Godhead, words cannot adequately express the pain and frustration of living in this fallen world. And the Spirit groans with us and through us and for us and carries those groans to God the Father.

And so verse 27: 'He who searches our hearts knows the mind of the Spirit, because the Spirit intercedes for God's people in accordance with the will of God.' The Spirit takes our wordless groans which we can't quite express and he carries them to the Lord in ways that the Lord can understand. He gets it. There will be a day when there is no more groaning. The groans lead to glory. We are hoping and waiting patiently for what is certain, and in the meantime we face up to the reality of suffering. Don't live below the line, but don't live above the line.

Truths about suffering

Four very quick truths about suffering from the verses we have looked at. Firstly, it can't be avoided. We saw that in verse 17: 'We are heirs – heirs of God and co-heirs with Christ, *if* indeed we share in his sufferings in order that we might also share in his glory.' There is no shortcut to glory that bypasses the groans. Just as Christ went via the cross, so we must suffer too. Part of the suffering is the agonizing process of putting to death the misdeeds of the body, as we saw yesterday. Then there are the general sufferings of living in a fallen world. It can't be avoided, so expect it. There may be some who have never really suffered in this life, especially some younger people, and we need to be ready for it. It will come. Just shortly after one of my friends returned home from university, her father committed suicide. It was a terrible blow and totally un-expected. She came back a year later and was interviewed in church. She spoke very openly and honestly about how terrible it was. But she also said, 'I'm so grateful that the Bible was taught to me while I was here, so I was expecting that at some stage in life suffering would come. It didn't make it easy. But I didn't feel as if somehow something that

I shouldn't have expected happened, because the Bible says that we can expect suffering.' She said to a congregation full of largely younger people, 'Can I just say to you, expect suffering.' We live in a fallen world. It can't be avoided. Not that we are seeking it, but it'll come.

But then secondly, wonderfully, it is under control. Verse 20 says, 'The creation was subjected to frustration.' It's under control. God has not been taken by surprise. Some people give the impression that there are two thrones in heaven – God sits on one of them and the devil sits on the other, and it's as if there is an ongoing fight between the two. Or maybe there is one throne, and they can't quite agree on who's sitting on it. Sometimes the devil wins and pushes God off the throne, and that is when terrible things happen in the world, and then God pushes back, and that is when good things happen. But the Bible says there is one throne in heaven and only one sitting on it, our Lord God, the Sovereign God. There is mystery, because the Bible tells us there is a devil who does terrible things, but God is in absolute control. As we'll see in a moment as we look at verse 28, he can even bring wonderful good from terrible evil.

The next truth about suffering is that it won't go on forever. Verse 18: 'Our present sufferings are not worth comparing with the glory that will be revealed.' And fourthly, we don't have to face it alone. Our Sovereign God is a God of amazing love. He sent his Son to die for us, he knows what it is to suffer and he sent his Spirit to live in us. The Spirit shares our groans and, as it were, takes them to the Father. So in the midst of suffering we can have great certainty.

Those are wonderful truths.

The certainty of the Christian

Let's look at the next section. We have seen the suffering of the Christian – now the certainty of the Christian (verses 28–39). It is true, there is great suffering and frustration, but there is nothing to fear: God will never let us go. There is great certainty for the believer.

The certainty of God's plan

The certainty of God's plan for a start. Verse 28: 'And we know that in all things God works for the good of those who love him, who have been called according to his purpose.' A very well-known verse, too often quoted glibly and out of context. For example, a husband whose wife has died, or you've just heard you've got an incurable disease, or someone you love has died: 'Oh, don't worry . . .' verse 28 is quoted, 'praise the Lord anyway.' It seems to make light of very real suffering. Not all things are good for Christians, and some things we experience are very bad indeed. Bereavement, sickness, heartache, the largely hidden pain of childlessness, unwanted singleness, a difficult marriage, the psychological scars of bullying, emotional or sexual abuse, the desperation of depression, addiction, estrangement from family or friends. All things are not good for Christians, and we are not expected to pretend otherwise. It's not that all things are good, but in all things God works for good, fulfilling his purposes.

The big question of course is: what is this good? Verse 27: 'The Spirit intercedes for God's people in accordance with the will of God.' The good is God's will which is described in verses 29–30: 'For those God foreknew he also predestined to be conformed to the image of his Son' (verse 29). This is his will for our lives – that we might be like Jesus once again, conformed perfectly to his image, perfectly reflecting his glory. The verse continues, 'That he [Jesus] might be the firstborn among many brothers and sisters. And those he predestined, he also called; those he called, he also justified; those he justified, he also glorified.' Those two verses span eternity. God has an eternal purpose for our lives and he will not let anything stop him from fulfilling it. That doesn't remove the pain, but it does give great perspective in the midst of it.

We have here in verses 29–30 what is sometimes described as 'the golden chain'. It begins, verse 29: 'Those God foreknew' – it is not speaking simply about the fact that he can tell in advance what choices we might make. It speaks about an intimate, personal knowledge. God set his love on a group before they ever loved him, before they were born. This golden chain is not fastened ultimately by anything I do – if it was, it would be bound to break. It is fastened on God's gracious commitment. Before I was even born, God foreknew and 'those he foreknew he also predestined'. Having set his love on a people, he decided on his plan for them and determined to fulfil it, that they might be conformed to the likeness of Jesus. 'Those he predestined, he also called' – it is not simply talking about putting out an invitation and nervously looking to see if anyone might respond. He speaks of listening to his voice – new life the dead receive – he calls his own. 'Those he called, he also justified', that we might be absolutely in the right with God. 'Those he justified, he also glorified' – there will be no more groaning. He speaks of it as if it had already happened, the so-called 'prophetic past'. It is as good as done, absolutely certain. It's guaranteed. He will keep us all, all the way. None will fall out.

Now of course there is great mystery in this wonderful teaching about God's sovereignty, and let's be clear, it does not deny human responsibility. Maybe you are not a Christian, and God appeals to you to repent and believe. You know the old illustration that as you walk towards an arch, you see a text above it saying, 'Come to me all who labour and are heavily laden.' You make the choice to come to Christ, you go through the arch and turn around and see on the other side of the arch a different text which says, 'You didn't choose me; I chose you from before the creation of the world.' But this doesn't deny human responsibility. It doesn't excuse human passivity – 'Oh, God's got his own; he'll bring his own in, so I don't have to bother to pray; I don't have to bother to tell the world. We don't have to bother to go out and be missionaries.' God uses means, he uses the prayers of his people, he uses the faithful preaching and proclamation of his people.

But I can be sure that if I put my trust in Christ, I will be born again. The Spirit of God is in me, giving me a new heart, a new desire to please him, even though I don't do it as I should. I have a new intimacy, a sense that I'm a child of God; I can be sure I'm justified and I will be glorified. Whatever happens in my life, I can be sure that all things work for good, because all things lead to glory. Terrible things may happen, but God is at work and forming us into the likeness of Jesus. Of course there is mystery: 'Why did God allow this to happen to me?' Or sometimes even harder to deal with: 'Why did God allow that to happen to him or to her?' when it's someone we love very much. It doesn't make any sense, and sometimes we don't see any good coming from it, but we can trust our Sovereign God that in all things he is at work, conforming his people into the likeness of Jesus Christ and ensuring that nothing will prevent us from ultimately getting to glory. There is the certainty of God's plan.

The certainty of God's protection

Next is the certainty of God's protection (verses 31–34). Verse 31: 'What, then, shall we say in response to these things? If God is for us, who can be against us?' We will have enemies. There will be those who don't like our Christian faith, and I think in this country we can expect that enmity to increase. I hope not, but the signs are heading in that direction. There may be other Christians who think we are much too narrow in holding on to the teachings of the Bible. We have got the enemy of the devil, but if God is for us, we have got nothing to fear.

Verse 32: 'He who did not spare his own Son, but gave him up for us all – how will he not also, along with him, graciously give us all things?' Maybe you are struggling right now. You are just overwhelmed with the difficulties of life. Your own sin, terrible circumstances, division within the church. Don't despair, God loves you. Do you think the living God who sent his Son to die for you – that's the hard bit if you like – will not finish the job and take you to be with him forever? He will not let you go. Verse 33: 'Who will bring any charge against those whom God has chosen? It is God who justifies.' Yes, we will fail. We will commit terrible sins, and there will be all sorts of accusers – the devil accusing us, someone we have wronged accusing us, even our own conscience accusing us. But however terrible our sin, the prosecution cannot win, because God has already delivered the verdict: 'Justified'.

Verse 34: 'Who then is the one who condemns? No one. Christ Jesus who died – more than that, who was raised to life – is at the right hand of God and is also interceding for us.' The moment we sin you can imagine Satan accusing us before God, and then Jesus Christ stands and says, 'Father, I died for their sin. I've dealt with it already. I faced your wrath, I faced the judgment.' Justified.

A young man came to see me not long ago, terribly convicted about a sin he had committed years before. He couldn't move on in the Christian life because he felt so wretched about this sin. He had never told anyone about it. He was so ashamed of what he had done that he said, 'I can't say it.' I said, 'Just write it down on a bit of paper.' He wrote it down and showed me. I said, 'Are you trusting in Christ?' He said, 'Yes, I am trusting in Christ.' I said, 'Do you believe Jesus died for you?' He said, 'Yes, I believe Jesus died for me.' And I said, 'He's dealt with it. You are absolutely clean before the Lord. Justified.' Then I got a match and I lit the bit of paper, and he saw it turn to ashes. Dealt with.

The certainty of God's love

The certainty of God's plan, the certainty of God's protection, and finally, there's the certainty of God's love (verses 35–39). Our sins cannot separate us from God's love – we've just seen that – and neither can our circumstances. Verse 35 begins with another question: 'Who shall separate us from the love of Christ?' Then he lists all sorts of possible candidates: 'Shall trouble or hardship or persecution or famine or nakedness or danger or sword?' Now why ask those questions if he doesn't imagine that these things could happen for Christians? Don't have a naïve spirituality that thinks, 'If I'm really faithful to God, terrible things will never happen to me.' Paul says, 'No, these things may happen. You might face every one of them: trouble, hardship, persecution, famine, nakedness, danger, sword (martyrdom in other words).' Christians loved by God can face terrible suffering.

He quotes from the Old Testament in verse 36: 'For your sake we face death all day long; we are considered as sheep to be slaughtered.' 'For your sake! We have been faithful to you, Lord, and it's because of our faithfulness to you that we are suffering, that we are like sheep to be slaughtered.' Suffering can happen not just because of the general circumstances of living in a fallen world; it can happen even because of our faithfulness to Jesus, and some of you have scars because of your faithfulness to Jesus. You are a pastor and you desperately try to preach the truth, but people don't like what they are hearing and they want to get rid of you. Or you are faithful to Christ at work, you stand up for him and people are giving you the cold shoulder. Or in your family you feel alienated. These things can happen. But when sufferings come, they cannot separate us from the love of God in Christ.

Now note verse 37: 'In all these things we are more than conquerors through him who loved us.' Literally, we are super-conquerors. Not *from* all these things, but *in* all these things. No doubt we will be battered and bruised, physically and emotionally, but we will come through because all things lead to glory. Meanwhile, all things work for good.

Verses 38–39:

I am convinced that neither death nor life, neither
angels nor demons, neither the present nor the future,
nor any powers, neither height nor depth, nor
anything else in all creation, will be able to separate
us from the love of God that is in Christ Jesus our
Lord.

It's a comprehensive list. 'Neither death nor life' – death may separate us from one another, but not from God; nor life with all its eventualities. 'Neither angels nor demons' – in other words, no spiritual force; they are powerless before Christ. 'Neither the present nor the future'. Maybe you are going through a bad patch now? You are lonely, depressed, discouraged. You may not feel God's love, but he is with you. What's your greatest fear as you face the future? Maybe the loss of friends, the loss of family, the loss of your job, the loss of your reputation, the loss of your mind? All those things can happen to you. You could lose them all, but in Christ you cannot lose God. 'Nor any powers', spiritual, temporal – oppressive regimes can deprive Christians of property and freedom, even their lives, but they cannot separate them from God's love. 'Neither height nor depth' – you can go up to the moon, go down to the bottom of the sea. Some of us are going back to difficult circumstances, maybe to a non-Christian family or a secular workplace, but it doesn't matter where you go, God is there. Then just in case he has missed anything, there is a catch-all phrase: 'nor anything else in all creation'. Nothing 'will be able to separate us from the love of God that is in Christ Jesus'.

The story is told that when the early church leader John Chrysostom was on trial for his life, he was interviewed by the Roman emperor. The emperor said,

'We will banish you.'

Chrysostom said, 'You can't. The whole world is my Father's house.'

'Well then, we will execute you.'

'You can't. My life is hid with Christ.'

'Well then, we will dispossess you of your estate.'

'You can't. All my treasure is in heaven.'

'Well then, we will put you in solitary confinement.'

'You can't. I have a Friend from whom you can never separate me. I defy you. There is nothing you can do to me.'

Other human beings may let us down, even the best of them. It's in Christ and only in Christ that we find the eternal security we long for. And when he says, 'I will always love you', he means it.

The soul that on Jesus has leaned for repose,
he will not, *he* will not desert to its foes;
That soul, though all hell shall endeavour to shake,
he'll never, no, never, no, never forsake.[2]

Notes

1. C. S. Lewis, *The Last Battle* (HarperCollins, 2009), p. 193.
2. 'How Firm a Foundation' (1787), author unknown.

The Lecture

The Apologetic of Evil – How Evil Demonstrates the Existence of God

by David Robertson

David Robertson is the Minister of St Peter's in Dundee. He is also Director of The Solas Centre for Public Christianity, a chaplain at the University of Dundee and a frequent speaker at student conferences and missions. David is married to Annabel, and they have three children. He is regularly involved in the media through writing newspaper articles, speaking on radio programmes and, more recently, doing some work for TV's Channel 4. David has also written four books. His hobbies are reading, music, history, politics, hill walking, languages, travel, films, football and cycling.

The Apologetic of Evil – How Evil Demonstrates the Existence of God

We are going to look at this question of the apologetic of evil. The simple thing I want to do is explain why people think that evil is a reason for not believing in God. I don't want to defend God; I want to say that evil is actually a fundamental reason *for* believing in God. What's often used as a reason not to believe in God is actually a reason to believe.

So, we begin by asking how we work out what evil is. Views of evil tend to fall into one of four opposing camps. *Moral absolutism* holds that good and evil are fixed concepts established by God or gods, by nature, by morality, common sense or some other source. In other words, there are things that are good; there are things that are bad. There are things that are true; there are things that are false. There are things that are right; there are things that are wrong. That is the Christian position. It is the position of most theistic religions and, to be honest, in their hearts, it is the position of most human beings.

Amoralism claims that good and evil are meaningless, that there is no moral ingredient in nature. *Moral relativism* holds that standards of good and evil are only products of local customs, culture or prejudice. So, for example, we would say that racism is wrong, but maybe that's just our culture. Maybe in another culture they would say that racism is right. Many people who are the governors in our culture would say, 'It's all relative.' You can see how that affects society. For example, take the question of same-sex marriage. Ten years ago, fifteen years ago, virtually no-one would have said, 'Well, yes, this is something that is obvious, right and fair.' And now, if you want a job as a politician or you want to get on the BBC and you deny this, you are some kind of weird, fascist homophobe. It does seem very strange how morality changes, and so people say, 'Well, yes, it is just relative.'

Moral universalism is an attempt to find a compromise between the moral absolutist view and the relativist view. It seems to me an impossible task, so I'm not going to waste time talking about it. If you happen to be a moral universalist and you want to explain it to me, then please feel free to do so. The position I'm working from is simply this: all of us have a sense of evil and a sense of good, and ultimately that comes from the image of God in us and the law of God written on our hearts.

So, here is the problem of evil. God is omnipotent, so he could destroy evil. God is good, so he would want to destroy evil. But evil exists, so the good, omnipotent God of the Bible cannot exist. Richard Dawkins describes it in this way:

> In a universe of electrons and selfish genes, blind physical forces and genetic replication, some people are going to get hurt, other people are going to get lucky, and you won't find any rhyme or reason in it, nor any justice. The universe that we observe has precisely the properties we should expect if there is, at bottom, no design, no purpose, no evil, no good, nothing but pitiless indifference.[1]

Now, that tells me that if you are not a Christian, if you do not accept there is a God, you still have a problem with evil. Now, I don't know about you, but sometimes as a Christian I lie awake and think, 'But Lord, what about this?' and 'Lord, why is this happening?' I get really distressed, but I would be in the pit of despair if I believed that the universe had no purpose, no good and no evil. If the problem of evil is a problem for the believer, it is an even bigger problem for the unbeliever.

Let me again explain it in this way: if you are an evolutionary naturalist, and by that I mean someone who not only just believes in evolution but believes that the material is all there is, then you have a real problem with the problem of evil. For example, you obviously accept there is no life after death, there is nobody to answer to, and once you die, that's it. So from the evolutionary naturalist perspective, there is no ultimate foundation for morality.

Morality is just something that has evolved. There is no ultimate meaning in life. What, after all, is the purpose of life if we are just going on from one meaningless existence to another?

There is no human free will, and that is a huge problem for the evolutionary naturalist. It means that I'm programmed to do certain things. It means that I can't be held accountable. It means that when I stand before a judge and he says, 'Why did you rape that woman?' or 'Why did you break into that house?', you reply, 'I couldn't help it – it's my genes. It's just the way that I am. I had no free will.' It takes away human responsibility. I grew up on a farm; my Dad was a farm worker, and he worked on a pig farm. Baby piglets are born blind and, until they open their eyes, you would not go near them. You certainly would not touch them. Why? Because if you did, the sow, the mother pig, would quite often eat her own piglets. Now, if a human mother kills her own children or eats her own children, she is going to court, she is going to be held responsible. We didn't hold trials of sows for eating their own piglets. It is ridiculous to have that concept, but part of being human is that we are responsible; we have an element at least of free will.

Friedrich Nietzsche wrote a book called *Beyond Good and Evil*, and he says this:

> We believe that severity, violence, slavery, danger in the street and in the heart, secrecy, stoicism, tempter's art and devilry of every kind, that everything wicked,

terrible, tyrannical, predatory and serpentine in man
serves as well as the elevation of the human species as
its opposite.[2]

You need to understand what Nietzsche was doing.
Nietzsche is the prophet of the nineteenth century whose
prophecies came true in the twentieth century. You
remember his saying that 'God is dead.' What most people
don't know is the second part of that quote where he
explains that God is dead and we have filled Europe with
the stench of his corpse. That prophecy came true in the
twentieth century. Sixty million people were killed. What
Nietzsche is saying is that all the things we consider to be
wrong, all the things we consider to be evil, in actual fact
serve towards elevating humanity, human progression.
In our culture you are aware of course that if you are a
politician, you have got to say that you are progressive.
Everyone wants to be progressive. Who doesn't want to
be progressive? I believe that what is happening in our
culture is not progression, but regression. We are regress-
ing from a Judeo-Christian view of the world back into a
pagan Greco-Roman view of the world. We are not
advancing, we are not human beings elevating ourselves
to a greater height; we are going down into the pit. Now,
Christians may want to despair at that, and we should
certainly be horrified at it. But don't despair, because where
did the Christian gospel first flourish? In the Greco-Roman
pagan world. That means, in my view, that we have got a
great opportunity to flourish again.

The problem with the atheist view of evil, apart from its consequences, is actually that logically it doesn't make sense and it requires a great deal of faith. I love C. S. Lewis's argument (forgive the lengthy quote) – he actually realized that the problem of evil was more of a problem for him as an atheist than it would be as a theist:

> My argument against God was that the universe seemed so cruel and unjust. But how had I got this idea of *just* and *unjust*? A man does not call a line crooked unless he has some idea of a straight line. What was I comparing this universe with when I called it unjust? . . . Of course, I could have given up my idea of justice by saying it was nothing but a private idea of my own. But if I did that, then my argument against God collapsed too – for the argument depended on saying that the world was really unjust, not simply that it did not happen to please my fancies. Thus in the very act of trying to prove that God did not exist – in other words, that the whole of reality was senseless – I found I was forced to assume that one part of reality – namely, my idea of justice – was full of sense. Consequently, atheism turns out to be too simple.[3]

Atheism is too simple. If you say, 'I don't believe in God because the world is unjust, because there is evil in the world', and you then say, 'but there is no such thing as evil', you are of course contradicting yourself. So, the argument that is used by the likes of William Lane Craig, simply put, says, 'If God does not exist, then objective moral values do not exist.' Actually, Richard Dawkins would agree with that. In *The God Delusion* he says that it is very difficult to have absolute morality without religion. Craig says evil does exist. Therefore, objective moral values exist, because we are able to say what evil is. That is to say, some things are really evil, therefore God exists. It is a very simple, straightforward argument. I think it makes a lot of sense.

However, the atheist often realizes that and says, 'OK, forget about evil as a moral concept; we are going to call evil *needless* suffering.' Some suffering you can understand – you get a needle in you when you are going to the dentist; you understand that. But they say there is some suffering which appears to be needless. Now that argument is quite easily defeated, because here is the big problem – how are we able to work out what is needless and what isn't? Who made us God that we can judge everything? This is what I find extraordinary in the faith of the atheist, because the atheist says, 'Until God shows me enough evidence, I won't believe.' They are presupposing that they themselves have the ability to judge the evidence, and we need a whole lot more humility. Who are you and I to think that we can sit in judgment upon God? Well, of course we are the progressive species; we are the people right at the top of the tree. But what if we are not? We are discussing a God that is way beyond the tree, and that makes a big, big difference. Tim Keller explains,

> Tucked away with the assertion that the world is filled with pointless evil is a hidden premise, namely, that if

evil appears pointless to me then it must *be* pointless. This reasoning is, of course, fallacious. Just because you can't see or imagine a good reason why God might allow something to happen doesn't mean there can't be one. Again, we see lurking within supposedly hard-nosed scepticism an enormous faith in one's own cognitive faculties. If our minds can't plumb the depths of the universe for good answers to suffering, well, then, there can't be any! This is blind faith of a high order.[4]

I think that the atheist ends up living by faith by saying, 'If I can't understand it, if I can't grasp it, then it cannot be there, there cannot really be understanding.' The Christian is not somebody who doesn't question and doesn't think. The Christian is somebody who says, 'Do you know this? I don't really know.' Here is the extraordinary thing – I remember when I became a Christian, I was like the kid in the paddling pool, going, 'I'm the king of the ocean.' Now, many years on, I feel like I'm the kid at the end of the ocean, dipping my toe in water. Not because of doubts and fears, but because there is so much more to know.

I know that many of you at Keswick this week are more mature – that's the expression I would use. The English holidays start next week, and there will be more families coming. I know everyone is always going, 'We need the young people', and so we do; my church is full of young people. But I tell you, what we need is older people. And those of you who call yourselves 'retired', you need to repent, because you don't retire as a Christian. You don't. Your wisdom is needed. Your experience is needed, and what is needed more than anything else is for you to teach the young whippersnappers like me that we don't know it all, that there isn't an answer that we can instantly produce for everything.

So let's return to the Christian view, because I think intellectually the atheist view doesn't make any sense. Now, I really enjoy reading, and I love reading the Church Fathers. Some of the stuff Augustine wrote is absolutely fantastic and really helped me with this question of evil. The argument is, did God create a perfect world and then get it wrong? Or did God create a perfect world which he allowed to go wrong? Did God create the devil? Well, this is Augustine's argument: number one, God created all things. No question. It's not that there is a good God and a bad God. It's not that the devil creates some things and God creates other things. God created all things. Number two, evil is not a thing. Evil is not created. Evil, according to Augustine, is the absence of good. Why would God allow that to happen? Why would God allow the devil, initially, and then human beings, to turn away from good? I think the answer has to be found in what it is to be a free creature, being able to love. Evil is the absence of good, and in order for human beings to be able to love, then we have to be able to choose. And if your choice is that you can do anything you want, you can have free will as long as you only choose good – that doesn't make sense. So Augustine goes on to say, evil is permitted by God. He did not create evil, but he permits it for the good. Let me give you two quotes. First of all this:

> In the universe even that which is called evil, when it is regulated and put in its own place, only enhances our admiration of the good; for we enjoy and value the good more when we compare it with the evil. For the Almighty God, who, even as the heathen acknowledge, has supreme power over all things, being Himself supremely good, would never permit the existence of anything evil amongst His works, if he were not so omnipotent and good that He can bring good even out of evil.[5]

Listen to me, if you are going to take anything from this lecture, take that last phrase. We believe our God is so powerful and so great that the most evil, sick and twisted thing could happen to you in this world, and he is so omnipotent that he can take that and turn it for good. Augustine then goes on to say, 'He judged it better to bring good out of evil than not to permit any evil to exist.'[6]

God has created the best of all possible worlds: a world in which human beings can freely choose. We did freely choose, and we fell, and God was not surprised at that. He knew, because, before the world was even created he had ordained Christ to come and be the Saviour of his people. God was not taken by surprise; he is never taken by surprise with anything. He created this world to be a vale for soul making. He created this life, the one in which we determine our eternal fate, this physical environment, so that we can grow and we can mature and we can think and we can determine our eternal destiny.

Let me return to the definition of evil. For the atheist, evil is suffering or physical pain. For the Christian, evil is the breaking of God's law. It is the universe going out of harmony with its Creator. Sin, ultimately, is the only evil. For the Christian, pain is actually not necessarily evil; some pains are actually really helpful. In fact, it would be dreadful if you couldn't feel any pain. Why? Because, imagine if you put your hand in a fire and didn't feel any pain, it would just burn off. Suffering as well, for the Christian, can actually have good consequences. I know we can be too trite, and we need to be careful, but sometimes we say with the psalmist, 'It was good for me to be afflicted so that I might learn your decrees' (Psalm 119:71). God's answer? Who knows what is best for us? Who knows the beginning from the end? Not you, not me. Only God.

My whole faith is based around certain parameters. There are certain things that for me, if I didn't believe them, my life would completely fall apart. One is this: God is just. The other is: he is good and the Giver of good and he is love. The devil will keep coming and saying, 'Did God really say . . . ?' 'What kind of God is that?' And so we end up saying, 'Well, I don't believe in this God.' But no, I have to believe. The Word of God tells me that God is good and just, and though I lie in the depths of Sheol, he is there with me. God knows. The bottom line for the Christian is God is omnipotent, he knows everything and he is good. The minute you let go of either one of those, you have been defeated by the devil. You've been captured. Never ever doubt the goodness of God and never ever doubt the knowledge of God. Always doubt how much you know and always doubt your definition of goodness. We know so little in reality.

When I was a young minister, twenty-four years old, I was visiting a place called Bruar and doing a Bible study there. A woman asked about suffering, and I gave a knock-down brilliant answer. I mean, when I had finished, I was like, 'Yeah, gotcha!' I finished the Bible study, and she went through to make tea and coffee, and someone leaned over to me and said, 'Do you know who that is?' I said, 'No'. And they said, 'That's Richard's mum. Richard was born as a healthy baby, had an injection which went wrong and he became a severely handicapped child. The BBC made a documentary about his mother giving up her work to look after him and all that went on.' I went through to the kitchen and I said, 'I'm really sorry – I didn't know who you were and I didn't realize you were asking out of your own experience.' And she looked at me, and she didn't patronize me, but said, 'That's alright, son. You'll learn.' People do not look for smart answers. You should look for answers, of course, but you are dealing with human beings. When you are going through pain, the last thing you want is some Christian that comes to you and tells you, 'Cheer up! All things work together for the good of those who love God.' That's not how it goes. We have to be pastoral on this.

For the Christian, our ultimate answer in terms of suffering is not answering, 'Why?' It's answering, 'What has God done about it?', and that is the cross. That's why the cross is so vital and so essential in all that we say and all that we do. To think that the God whose hands flung stars into space was nailed to a tree and the agony that he suffered. Why? To deal with, and to defeat, evil; the principalities and powers are nailed to that cross. That's what our God has done. The unbeliever says, 'There is probably no God, so enjoy yourself.' How does that deal with anything? You take God out of the equation, and evil is still there, and suffering is still there. Actually, what you are doing is taking away, not the cause, but the cure for evil and suffering.

Dostoyevsky said, 'Pain and suffering are always inevitable for a large intelligence and a deep heart. The really great men must, I think, have great sadness on earth.'[7] What's wrong with the prosperity gospel in all its forms is simply this: it's telling people that in this life you can be perfectly happy, you can enjoy everything and you shouldn't experience pain and suffering. I heard a man say once from a pulpit, 'Why have a Mini when God can give you a Rolls?' I didn't even know where to begin in tackling that blasphemy. If you are going to serve Jesus Christ in this world, then pain and suffering are inevitable for a large intelligence and a deep heart. Dostoyevsky got it right. How do we deal with evil as a believer? I just love at the end of *Lord of the Rings*, when Sam says, 'Everything sad is going to come untrue.' I really believe that. I don't know how, but I think it is extraordinary that we can weep in this life and know that God is still in control and justice will come.

Now I want to finish with some applications. First of all, *deliver us from evil in society*. I've been reading Ezekiel and Jeremiah. What is it talking about? It is talking about incest and injustice. It's talking about sexual immorality and the gross perversion that's occurring within our culture, and it's saying to us, this is nothing new. Do you know that right now there is a problem in New York? That they can't get enough dog chefs to cook banquets for their dogs, and people are starving in the world. Do you think God looks at this and thinks, 'I don't care'? Vaughan spoke yesterday about God being angry and how some Christians don't like that idea. Really? I want God to be angry at a world that is full of injustice and sin. I don't want a God who doesn't care.

In the UK we talk about Christian values, but please let me tell you this: Christendom has gone. You can't keep Christian values without Christ. Why are you surprised that non-Christians behave like non-Christians? That's the way it is. How do we fight the darkness? What is the solution? To moan, to complain, to shout, to scream, to stand outside with banners and placards? No, it is to bring Christ into the darkest places in our land, in our lives. By the way, sometimes we might like to say, 'People don't like the church, but they like Jesus, and if we are really nice, they will like us too.' Actually, the more Christlike you are, probably the more people will hate you. They crucified him, remember? He wasn't that popular and he promised us, 'If they have hated me, they will hate you also.' And yet out of that hatred God can change people's lives and hearts. Deliver us from evil in society; surely that is what we want.

Deliver us from evil in the church. Evil in the church? Yes, there is a real spiritual battle in the church. Peter confessed Jesus Christ, and then immediately Jesus was saying to him, 'Get behind me', because the devil was using Peter to undermine the work of Christ. My problem is not the godless society I live in; my problem is the pettiness, the triviality, the superficiality, the false doctrine, the false teaching, the ignorance, the arrogance, and the pride amongst the Lord's people. Not just in the liberal church, but in the evangelical church. I want to say this to you: you will never get anywhere until you recognize the evil that exists within your own church. And when we cry, 'Deliver us from evil', when Jesus comes to do that and to bring glory into his church in renewing grace and loving power, you know what will happen? You and I will fall at his feet as though dead, because when the darkness of our own hearts, when the corruption of our churches, is exposed before the glory and purity of his light, we will be stunned.

Some of you are here and you are so discouraged by the church. Please be discouraged because it shows you feel with the heart of Christ. But please don't think, 'Oh, it's all lost.' It's not all lost, because it's not all about you and it's not all about me; it's about Christ, and 'He will build his church and the gates of hell will not prevail against it.' But please be aware that when you are praying for revival and renewal, it is not going to begin out there; it is going to begin in here. Peter says, 'Be alert and of sober mind. Your enemy the devil prowls around like a roaring lion looking for someone to devour. Resist him, standing firm in the faith, because you know that the family of believers throughout the world is undergoing the same kind of sufferings' (1 Peter 5:8–9). Was it not Spurgeon who said that he could handle the devil; it was the deacons he had trouble with? There are some of us who know what that is like.

Deliver us from evil in me. Joseph Conrad's *Heart of Darkness* was made into the film *Apocalypse Now*. I think it is a brilliant book that shows the deep darkness that is within humanity. I'm not going to just feel the evil that is in society, and you must feel that, and I'm not just going to feel the evil that is within the church, because we must see that too. I have to look in the mirror of the Word of God and see the darkness that is within me, and I see that in two different ways. First of all myself: Christ came to save me, the chief of sinners. But secondly, in terms of spiritual warfare.

Many of you know that in 2011 I was seriously ill. I spent nine weeks in hospital, five of those weeks in intensive care, and I was given a fifty–fifty chance of survival. I think it was much worse for my family than me, except perhaps in one area. Without going into any detail, I experienced a spiritual blackness and a spiritual darkness that I have never in my life experienced and I never want to experience again. I know that for many believers, there is depression, darkness and discouragement. Spurgeon had it; M'Cheyne had it. Have you ever had that as a Christian? Have you ever had that experience of dread? Worn out, discouraged, but beyond that – spiritually, you are in darkness. So much so, that you can understand why even Christians commit suicide. 'Who will rescue me from this body that is subject to death? Thanks be to God, who delivers me through Jesus Christ our Lord!' (Romans 7:24–25); 'Even though I walk through the darkest valley, I will fear no evil, for you are with me; your rod and your staff, they comfort me' (Psalm 23:4). Psalm 91: 'You will not fear the terror of night . . . He will call on me, and I will answer him; I will be with him in trouble, I will deliver him and honour him' (verses 5, 15). I love that psalm, and I loved it even more in hospital when I was in a coma and in and out of consciousness. There is an Australian band called Sons of Korah. They have a musical version of that psalm, and when I began to get better, I couldn't go to sleep at night without playing it, because I knew what the terrors of the night were. Whatever terrors you face, to know God delivers you from evil is just the most wonderful, wonderful thing. I would never pray, 'Lord, show us the evil that is in the world', or 'show us the evil in our church' or 'show the evil in my heart.' Not to the extent that it really exists, because I think it would kill me. But I will pray, 'Lord, show me enough that I cry out, "Deliver me from evil."'

This Keswick is called *Really?* I want to urge you to get real. I hope you are not playing at Christianity. I hope that this is not just a nice holiday for you. I hope that you are not retired. I hope that you are not a young person who says, 'Oh, I'll serve God later on in my life.' I hope that you are not mucking around. There is real evil, real darkness; there is real despair.

I can think of a woman I met who lived in very poor circumstances. Her partner had died from a brain tumour. She had three teenage daughters. She was not a Christian. She too had a brain tumour, but she didn't want to go to hospital, and several times she collapsed in her home. I didn't know what to say to her when she came up and spoke to me. I just looked at her and said, 'Do you know, life is ugly.' She said, 'Yes'. I said, 'For you life is really ugly, isn't it?' And she said, 'Yes'. I said, 'What would you say if I told you that even out of the greatest ugliness there can come great beauty?' And she started crying. I couldn't offer her physical healing; I couldn't guarantee that, but I could pray for her. I couldn't offer her riches, I couldn't resurrect her partner, but what I could offer her was the beauty of Jesus Christ. Even the possibility of that being true made her weep and made her long. This is what you have to offer to people; this is how we fight evil; this is how we defeat evil. Not evil with evil, not with the weapons of this world, not with the weapons of the devil. But we say, 'Let the beauty of our God be upon us that everywhere we go we radiate Christ.'

Do you know around the streets here there are people who will come across Christians who are rude, arrogant and ignorant and yet are coming to a Christian convention? That's appalling. There are kids whose fathers will go to church and be so holy and pious, and then when they go home, all the kids see is ugliness. Isn't that terrible? We want the beauty of the Lord our God to be upon us. Please pray that. Pray that God will deliver us from evil in our society, in our nation. We want revival and renewal. Pray that God will deliver us from evil in our churches. 'Lord, what a mess we are in! What blasphemy we have committed in our churches. What heresy, what false teaching, what wrong practice, what pettiness and selfishness we have indulged.' We ask for God to deliver us from evil and ask to be delivered from evil in our own hearts, but that only comes when the beauty of Christ comes upon us.

Notes

1. Richard Dawkins, *River out of Eden: A Darwinian View of Life* (Phoenix, 2001), p. 155.

2. Friedrich Nietzsche, *Beyond Good and Evil* (The Big Nest, 2013), p. 41.

3. C. S. Lewis, *Mere Christianity* (1952; William Collins, 2012), pp. 38–39.

4. Tim Keller, *The Reason for God* (Hodder & Stoughton, 2009), p. 23.

5. The Bishop of Hippo St Augustine and Thomas S. Hibbs, *The Enchiridion on Faith, Hope and Love* (Gateway, 1996), p. 11.

6. Ibid., p. 33.

7. Fyodor Dostoyevsky, *Crime and Punishment* (Wordsworth, 2000), p. 226.

The Addresses

What Do We Really Need?

by Becky Manley Pippert

Becky is recognized internationally as a speaker, an author and an evangelist. She and her husband, Dick, are the founders of Saltshaker Ministries, a global evangelism training ministry. For the past five years they have lived primarily in the UK in order to minister widely in Europe. Becky is the author of many books, including *Out of the Saltshaker* and her newest Discipleship series: *Live – Grow – Know*. They have four adult children and one granddaughter.

What Do We Really Need? Mark 2:1–12

To interpret Scripture accurately, we need to remember that *context is king*. What then is the context of our story? Jesus' reputation and popularity have clearly preceded him. When he returned to his ministry headquarters in Capernaum, a large crowd gathered. Not only local people, but Pharisees and teachers of the law who had come from Galilee, Judea and Jerusalem.

Why have so many people come to this particular event to hear him teach? It appears that it was a planned event, a formal investigation, to test his orthodoxy. The implication is that they have come to listen in order to report back to the religious authorities any unorthodox practices or teaching of Jesus.

So, the crowd gathers with all the credentialled religious authorities being seated inside the house, and an equally large crowd outside. Yet the story focuses not on the religious authorities, but on a man who has no name. We know nothing about this paralytic. We don't know how he became friends with the four men who brought him. We never hear him speak. We never even hear his friends speak. Furthermore, this paralytic would have had zero esteem in the eyes of the religious authorities. They believed that to be disabled was the consequence of one's own sin or the sin of one's family. So, as the crowd gathers, Jesus begins to preach the Word of God. That's the context.

The interruption: Mark 2:3–5

The first portion of this passage is about the interruption of the four friends and the paralytic.

Imagine the expectation and excitement of these four men as they carried this paralytic in what would have been a makeshift bed. Then imagine they arrived at the house, only to realize they couldn't get in because of the crowd. Mark tells us that they tried to take him into the house, but 'they could not get him to Jesus because of the crowd' (verse 4). What this suggests is that the crowd wouldn't make way for this man. Why? Because he was a nobody.

Now, first-century houses were usually a single storey with a flat roof. The roofs were made of clay or earth, and the houses normally had an outside narrow stairway that led up to the roof. Wouldn't you think, when they realized no-one was going to make way for the paralytic to enter, that they'd conclude, 'It's hopeless. We'll have to try another time.' But what an enterprising group of men! They must have discussed the situation with one of them, no doubt, saying, 'Look, there's no way we can get him through the front door. So why not carry him to the roof on the outside stairs?' 'Yeah, but once we're on the roof, then what do we do?' another might have asked. 'Well, let's dig a hole and drop him down!' 'Brilliant!' another responds.

Wouldn't you love to have seen the face of the paralytic at that point? What must he have been thinking? 'What if they drop me going up the stairs? What if one of the ropes breaks? What if one of them loses their grip?' Yet we never hear the paralytic say one word of protest. He was willing to risk everything to get to Jesus.

Verse 4 says, 'They made an opening in the roof above Jesus by digging through it and then lowered the mat the man was lying on.' What does this tell us about the four friends? They had one goal: *We must get our friend into the presence of Jesus.* They were certain of two things: they had a friend who was suffering, and Jesus heals. So somehow they had to find a way to get the two together. They were willing to risk embarrassment, being looked down upon by the religious elite, even having to pay to repair the roof. What remarkable faith they had, not only in Jesus' power to heal, but in the Lord's compassion! The crowd may not have allowed this man entrance – but *they* knew that Jesus had compassion for the overlooked and marginalized.

What do we learn from these four friends? *The kingdom of God is all about loving relationships.* What Jesus made clear in his teaching and his lifestyle is that we are to love God and our neighbour as ourselves. Genuine Christlike love involves sacrifice, which must be evidenced in our discipleship and our evangelism. Just look at the tremendous effort those friends exerted on behalf of their needy friend!

But the lessons for evangelism are important as well. Just as we invest in the spiritual growth of fellow believers, we must also ask God, 'Who are the people in my life that you are seeking?' Remember, regardless of how well people 'clean up' on the outside, without Christ they are cut off from life's true meaning and purpose.

The second principle here – whether we are discipling believers or witnessing to unbelievers – is this: *We must bring our friends into the presence of Jesus.* But how do we do that with unbelievers? First, by establishing authentic friendships in which we demonstrate to them the character and love of Christ. Second, we must invite them to read the Gospels with us. The greatest shortcut to evangelism is exposing our friends to the person of Jesus, because Jesus is irresistible! It is a big mistake to think, 'The Bible only speaks to us.' The Word of God speaks powerfully to unbelievers as well.

The spiritual healing

The second portion of this passage is the spiritual healing that occurs in chapter 2:5. What do you think the reaction of the paralytic and his four friends might have been when they finally reached Jesus, only to hear Jesus say, 'Son, your sins are forgiven.' You can't help but wonder if they thought, 'Hello?! Perhaps you didn't realize it, but he can't walk. That is why we made all this effort, because we were hoping that you would heal our friend!'

But what did Jesus see in these men? He saw they had faith in his power to heal. So what did Jesus do? He honoured their faith and expanded it into something much deeper. They arrived absolutely convinced that Jesus could heal, but they left realizing, 'This man can even forgive sins!' In other words, faith is a process, and this is true for believers as well as seekers. So we must be patient with both groups. Nobody gets it all at once. That is why, by the way, it's so important that we read Gospel stories with seekers over a period of time, so they can discover for themselves who Jesus really is.

But let's not miss something very important. The fact that Jesus forgives the paralytic before he heals his paralysis tells us something profound. Our deepest problem is not our immediate need. What Jesus seems to be saying to the paralytic is: 'You want me to heal your immediate need, and I'll do that, but you have a far deeper need that I must address for you to be truly free.'

This is a critical aspect of this passage, because we see that Jesus alone has the *real cure* for the *real problem*. We tend to think, 'If I could just get that job', 'if I could just marry that person', 'if I could just get a raise . . . I'd be happy'. The Lord takes seriously our human needs. But Jesus Christ came from heaven to solve the deepest need of all, that we are separated from God because of sin.

The Bible often uses the image of paralysis as a metaphor for being separated from God by sin. With this understanding, we see that the paralytic's story is everyone's story, because all of us have sinned and fallen short of God's glory. All of us are paralysed until we come to Christ by faith and repentance. Still, even though our unconfessed sin may separate us from God's presence, there are still many things a paralytic can do! He may talk with his friends, read a good book, listen to music. But the one thing he can't do is walk with God.

Think of the power of the symbolism in this passage! What do we do when people die? We have a funeral. What do we do at a funeral? We lower the casket into the grave with four pall-bearers. This story has all the symbolism of a funeral for a dead man. But it also shows us the power of Christ who came to seek and save the lost! As one author writes, 'The Bible isn't a script for a funeral service. It's always God bringing life where we expected to find death!'

What are we to learn from this part of the passage? *The world is incapable of helping us at our core need. Only the gospel answers our deepest need.* The world can offer political solutions, money, grants, education, all of which have a place, but the world can't help us at our deepest need. Why? Because our core problem is that we are separated from God.

That means we must resist the temptation to offer *only* what the world offers for a cure. Instead, we must *declare* the good news and *demonstrate* the application of the good news in all areas of life at the same time. For example, if we only address the 'justice issue' and say to the paralytic, 'Listen, I'm going to raise money and give you paid holidays so you will never have to beg another day in your life. And I'll see to it that you have food in the fridge. OK, now . . . walk!' He won't be able to do it. He can't walk because he is separated from God. He could receive all those wonderful benefits, but it would not solve the core problem of his life. That doesn't mean we must not address the issues of injustice. Indeed, we are commanded to care for the poor, to bring help in all the areas that have been damaged by sin. But if we fail to address the deepest problem of all – our estrangement from God – we will leave people fed but dead.

What if we offer the psychological or self-help cure? What if we say, 'My friend, you look depressed, and I know what's wrong with you. Your paralysis is the result of low self-esteem. You need therapy and to get in touch with your wounded inner child. Frankly, I think you also have some rejection issues. You must learn to say to yourself, "My paralysis isn't a problem to be conquered, but an opportunity to overcome!" Here are some self-help books and so now . . . Walk!' But he can't do it. All the therapy and self-help books in the world can't help that man walk with God. He is cut off from a God who loves him and who wants to be in relationship with him. The world can provide relief, but only Jesus provides the real solution for the real problem. That is the unique mission Christians have been given – the solution that no-one else can give!

The controversy

Thirdly, there is the controversy of Jesus. How did the religious leaders respond to Jesus' pardon of sin? Jesus discerned what they were thinking, which in essence was: 'Who do you think you are? God or something? This is blasphemy!' What the religious leaders correctly perceive is that by pardoning the man's sin Jesus is indirectly claiming to be divine. Those Jewish theologians understand that God forgives a repentant sinner. But what Jesus says is absolutely startling. Jesus says he could personally release this man from the guilt of sin.

Let's give these religious authorities credit for picking up on the theological implications of what Jesus was saying. No-one in the Old Testament, not a priest, not a prophet, not a theologian, was ever given that kind of authority. But the Lord pronounced forgiveness in his own name! The religious leaders knew precisely what he was claiming. This is the first passage where we see the religious leaders labelling Jesus a blasphemer.

What was Jesus' response? 'Oh, I'm sorry, you seemed to have misunderstood, because that's not at all what I meant.' Far from it! Nor did Jesus say, 'Listen, if you guys would just study your Bibles, you could do this too!' No, Jesus said he had the authority to pronounce absolute forgiveness of sins, and 'the way I will prove it is I'm going to heal this man, which you can see, which will verify the other miracle that I just did – forgiving his sins – which you can't see.' The Pharisees and the teachers of the law understood exactly what Jesus was saying.

These theologians were so much more perceptive about what Jesus was actually claiming than our modern responses. What do we often hear today? 'Oh, I think Jesus was a wonderful man and a wonderful teacher, just not the Son of God.' But as C. S. Lewis has made clear, how could Jesus be a great teacher if he was so confused about the main subject of his teaching? Namely himself.

What do we learn here? *When unbelievers are exposed to the real Jesus of the Gospels, their sentimental opinions about him are quickly corrected!*

The physical healing

The last portion of this story is the physical healing. What does Jesus say? ' "I want you to know that the Son of Man has authority on earth to forgive sins." So he said to the man, "I tell you, get up, take your mat and go home." He got up, took his mat and walked out in full view of them all' (verses 10–12).

The paralytic believed in Jesus, and Jesus forgave his sins, which is what allows our walk with God to begin. But Jesus also offered him a new start, a new beginning, a brand-new life. How we need Christ's forgiveness! But we desperately need the abundant life that Jesus offers as well.

Why can we have absolute certainty that Jesus alone has the cure? Because Jesus endured the ultimate paralysis. He endured death so that we may have life.

The phrase 'dead man walking' was something American prison guards used to say to clear the way when they were taking a prisoner on death row to his execution. 'Dead man walking!' meant 'No hope, only death'. My friends, we have a Saviour who died and rose again, and who offers life where there is the certainty of death. We have been given the cure for paralysis! Let's never lose that picture of the paralytic walking, and no doubt leaping, and praising God. Let's never forget that God's intention is always to bring life where there is death. Let's not fail to offer the only cure that truly transforms human beings, the gospel of Jesus Christ.

I want to close with a story about someone very dear to me who was a 'dead man walking' – my father. I wasn't raised in a Christian home and I became a Christian in my last year of high school. The very first day of my conversion I felt God's strong nudge: 'Becky, I want you to go and tell your father what has happened to you.' And I said, 'Oh no! Anybody but my dad!' I love my dad dearly, but he was an atheist, the quintessential self-made man.

But I knew the Lord was telling me to do it, so very reluctantly I went to him and said, 'Dad, I've been searching for answers for quite some time. You know that I have been investigating other religions. You may not know that I've recently investigated Christianity. I now wholeheartedly believe it is true. I have become a Christian.'

Dad listened to me carefully and said, 'Thank you for telling me. But *why* are you telling me this?' I said, 'Because God made me do it! I didn't want to. But God wants you to know that he loves you and he wants you to know him.'

Being young, I then added, 'So, don't you want to become a Christian right now?' And he said, 'Becky, look at this (gesturing to our living room). Honey, Jesus didn't give me this. It took a lot of effort and hard work and a little luck. I just don't get this need for divine help.'

From that point on, I tried many times over the years to share my faith with my father. He grew to have great respect for my faith, but he never had a faith of his own.

Then he had a series of small strokes that affected his short-term memory, and eventually he had to be placed in a nursing home when he was only sixty-nine years old. My once strong, in-control, witty, razor-sharp father was suddenly dependent. It was crushing to see someone I loved so much become so vulnerable. I never stopped praying for him. And then one day I felt that same unmistakable nudge from the Lord: 'Go and tell your father about me one more time.'

And so I went, again as a reluctant witness. On the plane I began feeling very nervous and prayed, 'But Lord, what if I do it all wrong? What if I don't say it right?' Dad was in the early stages of Alzheimer's, and I agonized, 'What if he's having a bad day?' Suddenly, this amazing peace came over me as the Lord brought to my mind what had happened on the first night of my conversion. I felt the Lord saying, 'Becky, what happened the first night you became a Christian?' I answered, 'Oh my goodness, you asked me to share my faith. I totally forgot! It was thirty years ago.' Then I sensed the Lord saying, 'You may have forgotten, but I did not forget. Becky, just go and be a witness. I will do everything else.' That's the wonderful thing about evangelism – God is the chief agent; he simply uses us as his messengers.

When I walked into the hospital, the nurses told me he was having an exceptionally good day. When we finally sat down to talk, I said, 'Daddy, I don't know quite how to say this, but when you die I want to know you are going to heaven.' He said, 'Me too.' I said, 'Dad, do you know how you can be sure that you are going to heaven?' He shook his head no. I said, 'Dad, do you believe that Jesus is the Son of God?' He looked out of the window, and I could tell that he was taxing every brain cell to try to have this conversation. Then he said, 'Before, no. But now . . . I think so.'

I said, 'Dad, do you know that Jesus loves you?' He said, 'Hope so.' Then I said, 'Do you know how you can know that Jesus loves you? Because Jesus went to the cross and he died for you. Now Dad, I have to ask you a very important question. Have you ever made any mistakes?'

Now that may sound a bit weak, but one of my Dad's biggest objections to Christianity was that he'd have to admit he was a sinner. So I decided to use an easier word. When I asked, 'Dad, have you ever made any mistakes?' he looked out of the window for a long time and finally said, 'Yes, one.' And then he added, 'No, two.'

I love my father, but like all of us, he has made many more mistakes than two! Then I said, 'Dad, Jesus died for your two mistakes. All you have to do is tell Jesus that you believe in him and ask him to forgive your mistakes, which the Bible calls sin. This is what is called becoming a Christian. Is that something you want to do?' He looked out the window for a full minute. Then turning to me and with full comprehension, he said, 'Yes!'

Because of my Dad's difficulties in speaking, I said, 'Dad, I'm going to pray on your behalf. If you agree with what I am saying, then I want you to nod your head.' He took my hands, and for the very first time I prayed with my father. I said, 'Lord Jesus, I am coming to you on behalf of my father. What my dad wants to tell you is: I believe you are the Son of God.' Dad nodded his head. 'And I believe that you died for my two mistakes', and he nodded his head vigorously. But then I realized I had to stop. I tapped his shoulder and said, 'You don't remember this, Dad, but you were once an extremely successful business-man. You always used to say to me, "Honey, you've got to know how to close the deal." But I can't close this deal, Dad, you have to. If you believe in Jesus and want to surrender your life to him, then you must tell Jesus "Yes".'

We bowed our heads once again, and with complete understanding, my dad said in a loud voice, 'Jesus, *yes!*' And then he added, 'Jesus, I love you!' In my entire Christian life I never thought I would hear those words from my father.

I called the nurses a few weeks later and said, 'How's my Dad doing?' And they said, 'You won't believe it; he's like a new man. So peaceful, so joyful.' Less than two years later my father died. There is nothing to which I can attribute my father's conversion other than sheer grace.

But isn't that true of all of us? Were any of us any easier for God to convert than my dad? So let's not hesitate to share the good news of Jesus Christ! Let's go forth and share the only news that solves the real problem with the real cure. May we return to Keswick next year with stories of having seen dead people walking – and dancing – for the joy of the Lord!

Can Anyone Really Help?

by Ivor Poobalan

Ivor has served as the Principal of Colombo Theological Seminary (CTS), Sri Lanka, since 1998. A graduate of the London School of Theology (UK), he gained a ThM in Old Testament and Semitic Languages from Trinity Evangelical Divinity School, Deerfield (USA). He is currently working on a PhD in New Testament Studies from the University of Cape Town (South Africa). Ivor is married to Denisa, and they have two daughters, Anisha and Serena. His other interests are song writing, rugby and Sri Lankan cricket.

Can Anyone Really Help? Mark 5:1–20

The story is about the heavily demon-possessed man whom Jesus encountered in the region of the Gerasenes. Our topic is: 'Can anyone really help?'

A man was enjoying a holiday in the mountains. One morning he was taking a walk, enjoying the spectacular scenery, and he didn't realize that he had got dangerously close to the edge of a cliff. The next moment he lost his footing and fell over the edge. As he was falling, his flailing hands got hold of an overhanging branch, and he held on for dear life. He looked down at the sharp drop below, and looked up at the impossible face of the cliff, and then did the next best thing: he began to shout for help:

'Help! Is there anybody up there?'

After just a few moments of shouting, to his surprise, he got a reply: 'Yes'.

'Who are you?'

'This is God.'

The man had not been on talking terms with God for a long time, but business is business. So he asked, 'Can you help me?'

'Yes'.

'What should I do?'

'Let go!'

The man is nonplussed. He looks down, he looks up, and then shouts even louder, 'Is there anybody *else* up there?'

Thinking about our world today, I'm reminded about that man – desperately hanging on between heaven and the great abyss of personal, social and political turmoil that threatens to engulf us. The civil war in Syria and the plight of millions of Syrian refugees, the Korean ferry disaster and the Turkish mine disaster, the enormous social challenges arising from the European Union project, the school shootings in North America, the terrorism of Boko Haram in Nigeria, the frightening revelations by Julian Assange and Edward Snowden, the intense persecution of the church in Asia, Africa and the Middle East, and the rampant hedonism of Western civilization. Doesn't our world feel like that man hanging over the edge of the cliff? And we rightly ask, 'Can anyone really help?'

Mark was writing to the Christians in Rome. The Roman state was becoming increasingly more authoritarian and morally chaotic. Nero, the erratic and despotic Roman emperor, had instigated violence against the fledgling

Christian church. He had had some believers thrown to the lions and others he used as human torches to light up the gardens for his parties and orgies. In that wave of persecution, the apostle Paul had been beheaded and the apostle Peter had been executed by crucifixion. The church had been driven literally underground; they were meeting in the catacombs. It was at such a time that Mark wrote his Gospel. It is a time of great adversity, when darkness appears to rule, a time when people were asking, 'Can anyone really help?'

How then does Mark begin his record? What note does he sound as he commences the writing of an entirely new genre? Mark 1:1 does not say, 'Things are falling apart, the centre cannot hold and mere anarchy is loosed upon the world', although that was true. He speaks into that situation, but he does not merely mirror his situation. Rather, he opens with the words: 'The beginning of the *good news* about Jesus the Messiah, the Son of God'. In fact, this would be his modest summary of the entire sixteen chapters of the Gospel of Mark: just the *beginning* of the *good news* of Jesus Christ the Son of God!

The setting of Mark's Gospel

Most scholars believe that Mark was the earliest of the Gospel writers. Tradition tells us that although his ministry had begun with Paul, he would ultimately be known in church history as Peter's interpreter. Peter had been killed during Nero's persecution, and the church in Rome must have felt quite distraught following this great loss. Mark's writing, it is thought, attempted to encapsulate what Peter had faithfully preached as 'the good news about Jesus the Messiah, the Son of God'.

Of the four Gospels, Mark is the shortest. With just 675 verses, it has fewer than John with 871. Matthew and Luke have over 1,000 verses each. But by virtue of being the earliest among them, Mark, in effect, has defined this new genre of literature. So a *Gospel* is a writing that focuses on the person and work of Jesus Christ in a way that aims to convince the reader that Jesus of Nazareth is indeed the Son of God who is now the Saviour of the world. And Jesus saves, not by the assertion of his power or by waving a magic wand, but by the passion of his humble, sacrificial death at the hands of his enemies.

Mark – and Matthew, Luke and John who follow him – are not 'biographies' that attempt to present a comprehensive picture of a person's life from birth to death. They are different. Gospels are disproportionate, giving extensive attention to the last few days of Jesus' life to highlight his humiliating, tortured, but sacrificial death and consequent resurrection. And, as a preface to this essential story about Jesus, we are given a few chapters to demonstrate and assert that the one who suffers and dies so is in fact the very Son of God who has come bearing the authority of God and demonstrating the power of God.

So the theme of Jesus' betrayal, arrest, torture, death and resurrection – in effect the unique Christian teaching about the cross – is introduced in earnest by chapter 8:31:

'He then began to teach them that the Son of Man must suffer many things and be rejected by the elders, the chief priests and the teachers of the law, and that he must be killed and after three days rise again.' This means that very nearly half the Gospel of Mark is focused on the death of Jesus.

Mark 10:45 condenses for us the essence of the Son of God's mission in the world: 'The Son of Man did not come to be served, but to serve, and to give his life as a ransom for many.'

The setting in Mark 4:35 – 5:43

The story of the demon-possessed man belongs to a cluster of miracle stories. Mark 4:35 – 5:43 reports four amazing miracles of Jesus in succession: the stilling of the storm, the deliverance of the demon-possessed man, the healing of the woman with the issue, and the raising of a twelve-year-old girl from death.

Together they constitute the most pernicious primal fears that lurk in the human soul: the fear of *disaster*, the fear of the *demonic*, the fear of *disease* and the fear of *death*. Mark shows us that Jesus has authority and power over them all.

Jesus can help, and Jesus does help in each of these instances. The most he uses to help is a few words. To the storm he says, 'Quiet! Be still!'; to the demon-possessed man he says, 'Come out of this man, you impure spirit!'; to the twelve-year-old girl, 'Little girl, get up!' In the case of the woman, Jesus does not even get a chance to *say* anything; she touches just the hem of his clothing, just the hem, and she is completely healed!

Jesus can help, and Jesus wants to help humanity in its most desperate needs!

What's the big idea? Mark 5:1–20

Mark's Gospel records for us eighteen miracles of Jesus, of which the restoration of the demon-possessed man among the Gerasenes is by far the longest account, requiring twenty verses. Why does Mark go into greater detail with *this* story? In fact, Matthew relates this story in seven verses (8:28–34), and Luke says it in fourteen verses (8:26–39).

Is it possible that, with this particular story, Mark sees the potential to illustrate to his readers the essence of the public ministry of Jesus? Did this event have all the elements to explain what was involved in the saying of Jesus: 'The Son of Man did not come to be served, but to serve'? How might Mark have expected this narrative of the demon-possessed man to help his readers? What lessons could they draw from it? An overview of Mark 5:1–20 immediately tells us that this is a very comprehensive account. It's like a short play with four quick scenes. In the first and the last, Jesus has an encounter with the man possessed by demons (5:1–9 and 18–20); in the second Jesus encounters the demons (5:10–13); and in the third Jesus encounters the people of the Gerasenes (5:14–17). Looking at them individually and taking them together, we may ask what is the main point Mark is trying to drive home? What's the big idea? It is that:

Jesus' commitment to help people demanded his personal involvement, exercised his spiritual authority, resulted in society's reaction, and opened the way for gospel engagement.

What does this story show us about the ministry of Jesus, and how can its lessons guide our thinking about following Jesus today?

Jesus chooses personal involvement rather than chasing political appeal (5:1–5)

Jesus sails into a messy situation. The region of the Gerasenes was not kosher; the people were a mixed population of Jews and Greek-speakers (who had settled there after the period of Alexander the Great), and they were not too committed to the Jewish way of life. The fact that they had herds of pigs numbering 2,000 tells you just how un-Jewish they must have been. In addition, there is a man running wild and naked among the tombs, screaming and cutting himself. Did Jesus know what he was getting into? I would have taken one look at the situation and thought of reboarding my boat out of there! But not so with Jesus.

In verses 3–5 Mark gives us a whole lot of details about this man. He was *unsociable* – he lived among the tombs and on the mountains; he was *uncontrollable* – no-one and nothing could bind him; he was *violent* – he tore off the chains and smashed them; he seemed to be in *perpetual torment* – screaming night and day; and he was *self-destructive* – cutting himself with stones. This is not exactly the setting in which we would like to spend a Sunday afternoon. But 'The Son of Man did not come to be served, but to serve, and to give his life as a ransom for many.' And his understanding of serving meant total, personal involvement; it was about getting himself into the very stuff of life in the raw; it was about looking away from himself to the needs of the other. And anyone could see that the Gerasene man was in a desperate state of need.

In the first century, people were strongly of the opinion that there was an unbridgeable gulf between the heavenly and the earthly, the divine and human, the spiritual and material. The one was high and lofty; the other was low and base. Because of this view of things, once people began to recognize Jesus as the Lord of lords and the King of kings, they found it difficult to believe that he could have actually participated in the stuff of our human nature and allowed himself to be affected by the vicissitudes of our earthly existence.

So they came up with a clever idea called 'seemingly so'. They said Jesus only *seemed* human: he *seemed* to be one like us; he *seemed* to suffer hunger pangs; and it only *seemed* like our human problems affected him. In reality, he was fully divine and felt nothing of our pain. Since the Greek word for 'seemingly so' was *dokein*, this heresy – which was roundly rejected by the church – was called docetism.

One of those who responded to this heresy was John the apostle. He countered this profoundly when he announced in the opening of his Gospel, 'The Word became *flesh* and made his dwelling among us' (John 1:14, italics added). The word 'flesh' had the basest connotation. It referred to our physical flesh, but also connoted corruption and weakness. John might have said that Jesus became *human* or that he acquired a *body*. Instead, he says, 'The Word became *flesh*.' Jesus ministered through personal involvement.

The Pharisees also believed in helping people, but their motives centred on themselves. Jesus says that when some people were helpful towards the needy, they announced it with trumpets in the synagogues and on the streets in order to be honoured by others. They were more interested in the political mileage they could gain from their charitable deeds.

Jesus would not help people for the cameras. He wasn't political. His compassion for this man was the motive. It launched him immediately into casting out the demons. Time and time again in the Gospels we see how Jesus is moved with pity for the needs of people. And when this happens, he doesn't form a committee, prepare a budget, or call the newspapers and TV stations. He simply gets in there to where the need is and ministers God's love and power.

Jesus exercises spiritual authority rather than expanding religious activity (5:6–13)

Another factor that shows itself most clearly in this story is the absolute power Jesus has over the demonic. He exercises spiritual authority.

The situation is unparalleled in the Gospels. This is the most number of demons found in one location. In fact, when Jesus asks, 'What is your name?', the man replies, 'My name is Legion, for *we* are many!' How many? Well, the fact that the demons called themselves 'Legion' is interesting. The term comes from the Roman military, where a legion typically referred to a unit of up to 5,400 soldiers! This man was not possessed by a few dozen or a couple of hundred; he had a few thousand demons inhabiting his being. But neither their numbers nor their powers fazed Jesus. John the apostle later wrote in 1 John 3:8, 'The reason the Son of God appeared was to destroy the devil's work.'

John 1:10 says, 'He was in the world, and though the world was made through him, the world did not recognise him', but not so with the demons. They knew exactly who he was, and they could recognize him from afar! In the Gospels we find that the demons were quite vocal. In Mark 1:24: 'What do you want with us, Jesus of Nazareth? Have you come to destroy us? I know who you are – the Holy One of God!' Even in Mark 5:6–7 we see this reaction.

In recent times Christians have become more interested in and aware of spiritual warfare, recognizing that we do not fight 'against flesh and blood, but . . . against the spiritual forces of evil in the heavenly realms' (Ephesians 6:12). But with our increasing interest in the demonic, it appears that we have also increased our fear of the demonic. We have come up with novel ideas about spiritual warfare, and for a couple of decades Christians around the world were drawn into hunting down demons using spiritual-warfare techniques. We began to believe that we were besieged by demons, and the only way we could stay protected was by regularly and intentionally 'covering [ourselves] by the blood'! So 'cover with the blood' became a kind of mantra applied not only to oneself and family members, but to the house, the meeting places, even the cars and buses we travelled in! What we forget is that in Christ we don't find techniques against the devil; we find spiritual authority. Not only is Jesus fully endowed with spiritual authority; he freely grants that same authority to his disciples (Luke 10:17–20).

Isn't it telling that the demons (a legion of them) are 'begging' Jesus for something? That is spiritual authority. It comes to us by grace, and grows as we grow in our walk of faith. But sometimes we want a more visible authority, one that will impress people. This is what drove the church down the ages to develop external symbols of spiritual authority like special clothes, accessories, artefacts, and architecture of church buildings. We didn't care about having authority over the enemy; we simply wanted to look like we had authority. So, like the Pharisees of Jesus' day, we began to focus on our religious activities that would secure our sense of importance. As Paul says, 'having a form of godliness but denying its power' (2 Timothy 3:5). In Ephesus there were the seven sons of Sceva who wanted to cast out a demon (Acts 19:13–16). They thought it all depended on having the right technique and the right incantation: 'In the name of the Jesus whom Paul preaches, I command you to come out.' The demon's answer tells us a lot about spiritual authority: 'Jesus I know, and Paul I know about, but who are you?' The possessed man beat the seven and chased them out naked and bleeding!

Jesus coped with society's reactions rather than compromising into cultural accommodation (5:14–17)

We mustn't be naïve: the gospel divides. It brings joy to those who believe, but often provokes discomfort and even anger among those who refuse to believe. Sometimes Christians fear this reaction and try to mitigate it by becoming as winsome as we can be. We become political; we accommodate ourselves to our cultures. We say nothing different, we do nothing different, we want to show no difference, and in the end we make no difference!

Jesus knew that when he helped to restore this tormented man and sacrificed the thousands of pigs, he would be provoking a social reaction. But he did not compromise. In this case the gospel had struck a blow to the economy of that community: 'Those who had seen it told the people what had happened to the demon-possessed man – *and told about the pigs as well*' (verse 16).

Their reaction is curious. They are afraid, and they are desperate for Jesus to leave. They can see two things: a once crazily-possessed man is seated, clothed and in his right mind, and 2,000 pigs have drowned. One man: 2,000 pigs? Any more gospel and we might lose our economy. It's best to rid ourselves of Jesus!

Paul found this same reaction in his ministry, although far more violent. In Philippi (Acts 16) he is followed by a demon-possessed slave-girl whom he finally delivers. She had been an asset to her owners because she was able to foretell things for people, and so was a source of income. Now she could no longer do it. The huge commotion that followed – involving law-enforcement, magistrates, jail time and a severe beating – was all based on how the gospel affected the status quo, particularly the world of commerce. The same thing happens in Ephesus where the impact of the gospel cuts into the trade around the great temple of Diana. So severe is the reaction that it brought on a city riot (Acts 19).

In our personal lives and as Christian communities we can develop the great fear of what society will think. We fear opinions, we fear reactions, we fear threats, and so we are tempted to withdraw, to compromise and to look no different from anyone else. We are afraid to offend. But then the gospel can make no progress, and we will never see hopeless, tormented people enjoying the sweetness of their salvation.

In the UK, political correctness has become the new mantra. At times the imperatives of the gospel will go against the grain, and Christians and churches in the UK will have to say, like the apostles of old, 'Which is right in God's eyes: to listen to you, or to him? You be the judges! As for us, we cannot help speaking about what we have seen and heard' (Acts 4:19–20).

Jesus prefers gospel engagement rather than the promotion of Christian isolation (5:18–20)

Why does this restored man beg Jesus to let him go with him? His long period as a possessed man had made him a social outcast. He had been an embarrassment and had no friends. His family would have chased him out, so he had to live among the tombs. The society of the Gerasenes was hostile now to the one person the man could call his friend. He had no relationships to go back to. The thought of remaining in the region was unbearable. Wouldn't it be more prudent for this new believer to be with Jesus and become a *full-timer?*

But Jesus refuses. He prefers gospel engagement rather than Christian isolation. The man had been saved so he could become an instrument for salvation. Jesus was not permitted to remain in the region, but they couldn't prevent this man from going to his home: 'Go home to your own people and tell them how much the Lord has done for you, and how he has had mercy on you' (verse 19). The man was fired up, and he went away to preach in the Decapolis about what Jesus had done for him!

Conclusion and response

We began by looking at our world today, with all its challenges, and asked, 'Can anyone really help?' The story of the demon-possessed man in Mark 5 answers that question with a resounding 'Yes'. Jesus not only can help; he wants to help. And Jesus' commitment to help people demanded his personal involvement, exercised his spiritual authority, resulted in society's reaction, and opened the way for gospel engagement.

Is This Really for Me?

by Roger Carswell

Roger Carswell is a travelling evangelist. He leads evangelistic church and university missions as well as speaking at Christian conferences. He is a prolific author of gospel tracts, booklets and books, including *Things God Wants You to Know* and *Grill a Christian*. He lives in Yorkshire, is married to Dot and has four children and seven grandsons.

Is This Really for Me? Mark 8:22–26

I don't know who you would say is Britain's greatest-ever politician? William Wilberforce – how about that for a name? What a mighty man, the man who, under God, was responsible for the abolition of slavery. Of course, he came from Yorkshire and was converted to Christ as a Member of Parliament. Did you know he was responsible for starting the RSPCA and seventy other charities? He was the one who wrote to Pitt the Younger and said, 'You should come to Parliament.' They were great buddies all the way through their parliamentary lives, but William Pitt the Younger was not a believer, and Wilberforce was deeply concerned for him. He went to a church in Wimbledon, and it was announced that there was going to be a gospel service. So Wilberforce was very earnest in inviting Pitt to come to the service. They sat together, and

Wilberforce noted how clearly, simply, straightforwardly and challengingly the gospel was presented. As they went out of the church together, Wilberforce turned to Pitt, this brilliant man, the youngest ever British Prime Minister, and said, 'What did you think of what you heard?' Do you know what Pitt replied? 'I didn't understand a word the man was saying.' As far as we know, Pitt was never converted to Christ. The reason being, of course, there was a spiritual blindness in William Pitt.

The Bible says each one of us is born spiritually blind. We don't really grasp basic things: we are blind to who God is; we are blind to who we are; we are blind too to what God has done. I think so many people have the idea of God as a sort of finger-wagging God, telling us off about this and that and being out to get us. No, this vast God has loved us with an everlasting love, and there was a moment in time when God came into our world. God, big enough to become small; God, strong enough to become weak; this mighty God becoming as infinitesimally minute as a tiny foetus implanted in a virgin mother's womb in Nazareth nine months before he was born in Bethlehem. God came into our world, and he came with the express mission of going to a cross to die for us.

God wants us to know who he is, who we are and what he has done for us. He went to Calvary, and in those three hours of darkness when he was cut off from his Father, he paid for our sin. He was buried, and three days later he rose from the dead. Earth has never produced a greater victory than what happened in that garden when the tomb was empty and Jesus rose. God wants us to know, yet we are blind towards what we must do. Somehow we get the idea that if we could try hard enough and pull ourselves up by our own bootlaces, we might just earn enough brownie points to get us to God. We never will, we can never get up to God, but God has come down to us. He has taken the initiative and he wants us to turn from that which is wrong – the Bible calls that 'repentance' – and trust him – the Bible calls that 'faith'. Turning from our own way and turning to the Lord Jesus and trusting him for forgiveness and for new life. Yet people are spiritually blind to all these things.

There is a Zimbabwean proverb that says, 'Whoever ploughs with a team of donkeys must have patience.' It is a good proverb, and if Jesus is anything, he is patient. And interestingly, in bringing men and women to faith, to spiritual sight, he works according to our individual needs. He knows everything there is to know about each of us and he works according to where we are at. He will meet us at that point if we will allow him. God has his way with each individual soul. Isn't that wonderful? He knows us. He understands us better than we understand ourselves. He loves us, and he will work with us to draw us to himself.

Sometimes it is very sudden. I was converted suddenly. Somebody explained the gospel to me, I think for the first time ever, and I believed and was converted. It was the hinge that changed the whole direction of my life. But others come to Christ very slowly, and I am sure there are some here tonight and you are thinking things through. You are weighing things up, you are seeking, you are slowly edging your way towards the Lord Jesus Christ. God uses all sorts of means to bring people to himself. I know people who have been converted through sermons, through reading the Bible, through reading a tract, through dreams. My elder son works with university students in a church in New Zealand, and they have trainee students. The student he taught last year was converted through reading Richard Dawkins's book *The God Delusion*! He read it and he thought, 'If this is atheism, it has nothing to substantiate its arguments.' And he became a Christian.

Now, in Mark's Gospel chapters 7 and 8 we have two very unusual miracles. In both of them Jesus uses strange means to heal people. In both of them he uses spittle. I have preached in the open air and have been spat on. You put on a brave face, but deep down you feel disgusted and repulsed by it. Both men came from the same district, both were the same nationality, and in one of the incidents, the one we are going to think about this evening, this blind man was healed gradually. Now, that's all very unusual as far as Mark's Gospel is concerned, and as far as Jesus' usual workings are concerned. In chapter 7 Jesus healed a deaf man, but he healed him immediately after he had been speaking to people and calling them to hear and understand his Word. Now, Jesus has been speaking about spiritual blindness and he heals a blind person. Now, don't misunderstand, Jesus didn't perform miracles as signs only. In fact in chapter 8 he rebuked those who asked him for a miracle to 'show us who you are'. He healed out of a genuine heart of compassion. He had sympathy; he had love; he saw people's needs and he wanted to meet those needs and heal them.

Nevertheless, his miracles were parables of spiritual truth. And of course, all his miracles were also fulfilling what the prophets had been foretelling. Isaiah 35:5: 'Then will the eyes of the blind be opened and the ears of the deaf unstopped.' So Jesus was healing because he cared; he was fulfilling Old Testament prophecy, but he was also teaching a truth through what he was doing. So let's just look at how Jesus heals this man.

Secrecy

First of all, notice the secrecy. Some guys brought this blind man to Jesus, but he isolated him from them and from the people of the village. He deliberately took him away. Now, he had just fed 4,000 people, so it wasn't that he was averse to crowds, and we know the theme of crowds comes repeatedly in the book of Mark. But he took this man away from the crowds, and I think the reason was that the crowds were characterized by unbelief and cynicism.

Now, just a word, just a touch from the Lord Jesus Christ would have been sufficient to heal him, but that's not what Jesus did. He took him by the hand. Now, think about this – this is Jesus, the Lord of all glory, the Light of the world, who takes the hand of this blind man. It is not a handshake – there is something quite intimate. He takes the man's hand and leads him out of town. Now, this is really quite unusual. You can go through the whole of Mark's Gospel and you will see Jesus repeatedly insists on secrecy.

Strangeness

So first of all, there is the secrecy, but then as well I want you to notice the strangeness of it all. Jesus put his spittle on those glazed, diseased eyeballs. Why would he do that? He did it for the deaf man; why is he doing it now for the blind man? I think Jesus was entering the mind, entering the thought world of the man and establishing significant contact with him. So it was a touch, but it was a different sort of touch, and his mind would have been racing, and maybe faith was being stirred, and certainly there were questions being asked. And then, for the first time in years, the man saw light and colour, but it was only a partial miracle. Now, don't misunderstand, this wasn't an energy crisis from Jesus; it wasn't a sudden lack of power. No, this was a deliberate act of the Lord Jesus, because in Christ's eyes the man's faith was more important than his physical healing. It was more important that he understood who it was who was healing him than actually receiving the sight which one day through death he would lose. Time and again I've met people, and they've come to the Lord Jesus Christ gradually.

Slowness

Then notice as well not only the secrecy and the strangeness, but the slowness in which Jesus healed him. It is almost as if Jesus is accommodating the pace of his power to the slowness of the man's faith. In fact, as you go through the Gospel of Mark, one of his favourite phrases is 'straightaway', 'immediately'. There is rapid movement through the book. But on this occasion it wasn't an instant healing; it was slow, and I suspect that was because the man's belief was slow. He wasn't quite ready to absolutely trust in Christ; he wasn't quite sure that Jesus could do this yet, so Jesus accommodates the man's slow faith by this slow healing.

Clearly he hadn't been born blind. Blindness had come upon him later, because when he was seeing in a blurry way, he said, 'I notice some people, that is, they are indistinct like trees, but they cannot be trees because they are walking.' So he is seeing something, but it is vague, like when you are in an optician's chair, and they put these different lenses on you and ask you to read, but you can't because it's all a blur. Sometimes spiritual illumination comes very slowly, and Jesus stopped to accommodate that man's faith. Are you here with 1,001 questions? The Lord Jesus would never say, 'Stop your questions; just believe.' He will answer your questions, and there are answers to these questions. If you are thinking, 'I just don't know that I can take it all in yet', I would urge you to take one of these Gospels. Go to your room, your tent or your caravan, and just quietly read through and let the Lord Jesus Christ walk off the pages and reveal himself afresh to you.

Jesus gave him back his sight, and then he sent him home. It specifically says in verse 26, 'Jesus sent him home,

saying, "Don't even go into the village."' Again, I suspect
the reason for this is that the village was just cynical and
unbelieving, and so Jesus said, 'No, I don't want you to go
there. I want you to go to a place where you can grow,
relish what has just happened to you and think who did it
and why you have been so blessed.'

The story serves as a sort of dramatization of the spiritual
difficulty, not only of people of each generation, but
specifically of the disciples. Again, if you look at the whole
context, you will see this is exactly what is happening. Jesus
is concerned that he is with these disciples. He has been
with them day and night for quite some time now, but they
just hadn't got who he really is. They didn't see why he'd
come; they hadn't really understood his person and his
work. They hadn't understood that he was going to go to
the cross and die and rise again. It seems as though they
too had failed sight that gradually became partial sight
and eventually became complete sight. I'm not just making
this up: if you look at chapter 8:17–21, you will see Jesus
taking these disciples from non-understanding to misunder-
standing (8:29–33). The disciples are watching Jesus, living
with him, listening to him, sharing with him, and yet it is
all just beyond them; they don't quite get it. But then slowly,
they begin to understand a little bit more. They have still
got it all a bit muddled, thinking, 'Oh, he is going to come
as a great conqueror to rid us of the Romans.' And then
eventually, when Jesus has died and risen and of course the
Spirit has come to live within them, there is complete
understanding.

I want to ask you this evening, do you really understand who Jesus is? The one who is from eternity to eternity. The one who knows all things and can do all things and is everywhere. The one who never changes, who is the same yesterday, today and forever. The one who is absolutely just and yet loving, who is pure and holy. This is our Jesus; he is the God-man. Can I ask you, do you understand what he has come to do? His teachings have never been surpassed. People have sometimes said to me, 'Roger, will you just practise what you preach?' Jesus only ever preached what he practised. His words and his works were utterly consistent. There was no duplicity, no sham, no hypocrisy in the Lord Jesus Christ. So when he stood up and said, 'Does someone hit you on one cheek? Turn the other cheek', that is what he had been doing. 'Does somebody compel you to walk one mile? Go with him two miles' – that is what Jesus had been doing. When Jesus said, 'Love your enemies, pray for those who persecute you' – that is what he had been doing. Everything he said, he did, totally.

Those who scrutinized his life saw that he was totally faultless. John, very intimate with the Lord Jesus, said, 'In him is no sin.' Paul, the great thinker, the great intellect, said, 'Jesus knew no sin.' Peter, the man who was always doing things, said, 'Jesus did no sin.' The book of Hebrews, all to do with the old and the new covenant, said, 'He is without sin.' Even the enemies of the Lord Jesus testified in a similar way. Judas, who sold Jesus for thirty pieces of silver, cried out, 'I betrayed innocent blood.' Pilate, the man who was to sentence Jesus to be crucified, said to the crowd who were begging for his death, 'Why? What evil has he done? I find no fault in him.' Even the Roman executioner who witnessed many people being put to death by crucifixion said, 'This man was the Son of God.' They recognized that Jesus was different. The pure, spotless Son of God who went to a cross and took on himself my sin, your sin, the sin of the world, the sins which hit the headlines and the other sins which just harden the heart. Is there some sin that really dogs you, and you think, 'Oh, I wish that sin was laid on Jesus'? Is there some sin you look forward to? That sin was laid on Jesus too. He died so that we might be forgiven.

Do you know, the Bible says, 'He is the propitiation for our sins, and not for ours only but also for the sins of the whole world' (1 John 2:2 ESV). What is this word 'propitiation'? When you think about what is going on in our world, there is so much that must not only grieve the heart of God, but make this holy God angry, not in a sudden loss-of-temper type of anger, but angry at sin. Jesus is the propitiator – on the cross he took God's anger against my sin, your sin, on himself, and he did it because he loved us. Have you really grasped this? Have you got your head around the significance of the fact that Jesus not only died, but was buried and then rose, conquering the grave, conquering death? Sin has eternal consequences, but Jesus, the eternal one, in three hours paid for our sin. I don't know where you are at, whether you are totally spiritually blind at the moment, whether your eyes are just slightly open but you are not quite getting it. I'd love you tonight to have those eyes open that you might see Jesus as your loving Lord and Saviour.

A couple of hundred years ago in the town of Colchester in Essex an aristocratic gentleman by the name of Sir Roger Boulter was doing his business in the market square. He heard the town clock chime out the time. Like a child, he counted it – one, two, three, four, five, six, seven, eight, nine, ten, eleven, twelve, thirteen – the clock struck thirteen! He thought, 'Well, that was strange.' And as it happened, there was a guy standing near him, an unusual sort of faced man, but he turned to say, 'The clock struck thirteen', and Sir Roger said, 'Yes, I counted that as well. How strange!' And that was it.

Some weeks later he was at home in his beautiful aristocratic mansion where he lived. In the night he woke up and in his mind heard this strong, compelling inner voice saying, 'Go to York. Go to York. Go to York.' He tried to put it out of his mind, but when he woke the next morning, he thought, 'Go to York.' Eventually he just couldn't rid himself of it. He went to his men and said, 'Saddle a horse. We are going to go to York.' He made his way to the centre of York, and there were crowds of people outside the court-house. He went up to one of the people on the edge of the crowd and said, 'Excuse me, what's going on?' And the man just said, 'Oh, it's the last day of a murder trial, and we all want to know if the man is guilty or not.'

Well, Sir Roger Boulter was an aristocrat, and you know they can often get into places where most of us could never get. He pushed his way through the crowd, to the courthouse and up into the public gallery. He looked down and saw the judge was somebody he knew. Eventually, as he was watching and listening, the verdict came: 'Guilty of murder'. The judge, before he sentenced this man to be publicly executed, said to him (and Sir Roger still hadn't seen him), 'Do you have anything to say before I pass sentence?' And the man, in a pleading, earnest, desperate voice, said, 'Yes, I do. I did not kill this man. I was more than 200 miles away from the murder scene when it happened. I was in Colchester. There is a man who could testify to me because together we were in the market place, and we heard the clock strike thirteen, and I turned to him. If only I knew him!' And Sir Roger looked and said, 'Oh, there's that man.' And he put up his hand and shouted out, 'Your Honour, I am that man!' He made his way down and spoke to the judge. Eventually, the accused man was acquitted and walked out of the courthouse with Sir Roger Boulter. He was a free man, declared innocent, and rightly so. He turned to Sir Roger and said, 'Do you know, you are the only man in all the world who could have saved me.'

And I want to say with all the earnestness that I have, the Lord Jesus is the only one in all the world who can save us, and what we do with Jesus matters for all eternity. Do you know, everybody and every religion leads to God? The tragedy is that, for so many religions and for so many people, they will meet God as their Judge. But Christians will meet God one day as our Father; he will welcome us. Millions will meet God on the throne of judgment, but the Christian will meet God on that day on the throne of grace. But we can meet him today. Would you be willing to ask that your spiritual eyes be opened? Maybe they have been opened a little bit already. But would you ask for your spiritual eyes to be properly opened, widely opened. Would you be willing to pray, to call out in your heart of hearts, 'Oh God, reveal yourself to me. Please forgive me. Come and live within me, become my Lord and Saviour.' I beg of each one of you, don't leave this tent as somebody who is turning their back on God. If Jesus is taking you away from the crowd to touch you and give you back spiritual sight, then allow him to do so and trust him as your Lord and Saviour.

The Mind of Christ: Philippians 2:1–11

by Ian Coffey

Ian Coffey writes and teaches on the subject of leadership. He and Ruth celebrate forty years of marriage this summer – having met many years ago climbing in the Lake District. Four sons and seven grandchildren later, they claim to be older, wiser – and poorer! Ian and Ruth have served churches in suburban, city-centre and international contexts. They are now involved in training a new generation for servant leadership and speak at conferences across the world. Ian has an active interest in writing and has published fourteen books.

The Mind of Christ: Philippians 2:1–11

I wonder if I asked you tonight to describe your church at the moment, what would you say? Some of us have got some great things to say. We've seen growth, we've seen development, some exciting plans and maybe that wonderful thrill of seeing new people not only coming in from our surrounding community, but coming to faith in Jesus. For some of us, we've come away to Keswick this summer with a great deal of joy in our hearts for all that God has been doing. But for some of us, that isn't the story. It's been tough, and maybe you've come through, or at the moment you are going through, the hardest period your church has known. There have been challenging situations, difficult pastoral situations. There have been people you have prayed for, and the prayers don't seem to have been answered yet, or at least not in the way you would expect.

And there have been some tensions. There has been difficulty. There are folk within the congregation who are not happy and who are not talking to others. I wonder how you would sum up your church in a sentence tonight?

When Paul wrote to the Philippian church, they were about twelve years on in their faith. In Acts 16 we hear about the amazing growth and birth of that church, the first congregation we know of on European soil. But twelve years had passed. And you know as well as I do, that it is very easy even in the Christian life for things to become overfamiliar. And for those living as Christians in first-century Philippi there were many challenges. The culture around them was anti-Christian. Not just non-Christian, but anti-Christian. And some of those folk in the congregation at Philippi had lost businesses, friends and family relationships because of their decision to follow Jesus. And their beloved pastor, the founding pastor of their church, Paul, was in prison, hundreds of miles away in Rome. They prayed for his release, but he had got stuck in a legal logjam and had been in prison for something like two years, waiting for a personal hearing before Caesar. And they had kept on praying, but it didn't seem to make any difference.

They had sent one of their leaders, an elder called Epaphroditus, who had taken some goods, some money and some news. He travelled all the way from Philippi, probably involving a couple of sea voyages, to visit Paul in Rome, in order to share love, to tangibly express to him, 'Paul, we are with you.' And he got so sick, he almost died. He had that experience where you seem to be doing the right thing, and it turns out the wrong way. And so, when Paul wrote to his friends at Philippi, he was aware, because Epaphroditus had told him, that he was writing to some Christians who badly needed encouragement. And that's why this powerful little letter is packed full of encouragement. Fourteen times Paul mentions the word 'joy' or the verb 'rejoice'. Fourteen times in four chapters. Why? Because he wanted to get his friends connected up to the mains again.

I asked you to describe your church in a sentence. If we were describing the church at Philippi twelve years on from their decision to follow Jesus, three words would sum it up. They were dry, they were discouraged, and there was a very definite threat of disunity within the congregation. And in this thank-you letter in which Paul takes four chapters to get round to saying thank you, he frontloads it with lots of good things to remind his friends of what it means to be followers of Jesus in a hostile world.

In chapter 2 Paul writes to them about surviving in a local church. He writes about attitude, about getting along together, and as a wise leader, he knows that it is in the light of God's light that we see light. That's how he brings some truth to bear on a congregation that's dry and discouraged and in danger of disunity.

Look at yourselves

And in verses 1 and 2 he begins by saying, 'Take a look at yourselves.' He says, 'Take an honest look at yourselves and where you are in your journey.' Right at the very beginning of the reading, in most versions, not all, the word 'therefore' appears. In chapter 1 Paul has concluded by saying, you are in a hostile world, so stand together, one in mind, one in spirit, one in purpose:

> . . . striving together as one for the faith of the gospel without being frightened in anyway by those who oppose you . . . For it has been granted to you on behalf of Christ not only to believe in him, but also to suffer for him, since you are going through the same struggle you saw I had, and now hear that I still have.
> (Philippians 1:27–30)

'Therefore if you have any encouragement from being united with Christ . . .' And there are four 'ifs' in verses 1 and 2. One translator puts it this way: 'As surely as you are encouraged at being at one with Jesus, forgiven, set free. As surely as you find comfort from knowing that you are loved by him with an unquenchable, irresistible love. As surely as you have *koinonia*, fellowship with the Spirit. As surely as the Spirit is producing in your heart a tenderness and a compassion.'

What Paul is basically saying is: 'Friends, these are things that we believe to be true; these are gospel truths. Well, if they are, live them out.' And he says, I want you to be 'like-minded, having the same love, being one in spirit and of one mind' (verse 2). Can you understand for a church where there were tensions, where there were factions developing, what an appropriate word it was?

I often feel the word 'unity' in the Christian family is a bit like 'motherhood' or 'apple pie'. Everyone is in favour of them, but when it comes to the practice, it is something different. Have you heard the story of the group of Christians in a small village where they had three village churches? They decided after a period of time to merge into one. They were deciding which building to sell, which one to keep, even how they would structure their leadership as a church. The one issue they couldn't decide on was what to call themselves. And so they set up a committee – a good Christian way of solving things – and they met for about three and a half years. They considered all sorts of different options, including the 'Church of the Redeemed, of the Firstborn of the Seventh Trumpet Experience Incorporated', and thought, 'Nah, that's never going to fit on the letter heading.' In the end, someone, a young Christian on the committee, said, 'Why don't we just call it such-and-such "Christian Church"?' There was a stunned silence around the table. Then an elderly Baptist deacon cleared his throat and said, 'I've been a Baptist for forty-seven years; no-one's going to start calling me a Christian now.'

We get the point. There are times when we can make things of certain issues that are bigger than they should be. We major over minors. To use the analogy Jesus used, wonderfully humorous, we 'strain out a gnat but swallow a camel' (Matthew 23:24). We focus on the little things, and we fall out so often over very, very big things. Let me give you one subject that I'm sure resounds with you loud and clear: music. Charles Haddon Spurgeon, the Victorian preacher, writing in the nineteenth century, apparently said, 'When Satan fell from heaven, he landed in the choir stalls.' Now that must tell you something! If you look at church history, you'll find music has been one of the most contentious issues within the Christian church. Should it be that way? Expressing our worship and praise to God should surely draw us together, not pull us apart.

I was reading just the other day that the Church of England only authorized hymn singing in 1820 because it was such a controversial issue. And some have been brought up in traditions where there are folks to this day who think we shouldn't sing anything other than the Psalms. But do you see, we can often divide over issues like that? When actually they are much more to do with culture, taste, upbringing and personal preference.

Paul is saying through Scripture to his friends in Philippi, through Scripture to us today, to be careful that we don't major on minors. Be careful that we don't 'strain out a gnat but swallow a camel'. Look at yourself; look at what we profess to be: like-minded, having the same love, being one in spirit and in purpose. Look at yourselves.

Look at others

Then Paul goes on in verses 3 and 4 and says, 'Look at others.' How do we look at others? He says we must reject 'selfish ambition or vain conceit'. In church? Yes, in church! Selfish ambition and vain conceit are part of the old nature. One of the things I do when I prepare people for believers' baptism is to say to them, 'You know that when I baptize you, it doesn't make you perfect? I don't hold you under the water long enough for that to happen!' The only perfect Christian is a dead one – agreed? I'm not perfect; you're not perfect, so why do we expect perfection in one another? 'Selfish ambition, vain conceit – we've got to be on our guard against these things,' says Paul. As we look at others, we've got to judge our own hearts, allow the Spirit of God to unveil what our reaction is, because we feel they are getting preferential treatment; they are getting the limelight or the credit.

And instead of the selfish ambition, which is wanting to push ourselves forward, and the vain conceit, thinking more highly of ourselves than we should, Paul says, 'Embrace humility.' Verse 3: 'In humility value others above yourselves.' You know, in the world where the Philippians lived, their culture didn't see humility as a virtue. Isn't that interesting? Humility was seen as a sign of weakness. You were frail, you were someone who was pathetic and to be looked down upon. Yet here Paul is saying to his friends, be countercultural. Humility is a Christian virtue. Taking the lowest place, being willing to serve rather than to be served. In humility, he says, 'Count others more significant than yourselves. Let each of you look not only to your own interests' – isn't it interesting, he's not saying there ignore your own interests? That would be a nonsense statement. He says, 'Look *not only* to your own interests' – that's an understandable thing: wanting to survive, wanting to provide, wanting to look after those whom God has entrusted to us. But as well as that, look 'also to the interests of others' (ESV). Think about what is going on in their life. Look at ways in which you can bring encouragement and blessing. Don't always think the wrong thing.

One of the things that Steve Brady tries to encourage us to do at Moorlands College is to catch students doing something right. That's a good thing, isn't it? How do we catch people doing something right at church? I don't know whether you have folk at your church who look after the PowerPoint, the technical side, the sound. If you want to give them a heart attack, go up next to them and stand there and say, 'Thank you so much. I could hear everything, the band was just the right volume, and I really enjoyed the service.' That doesn't happen very often. 'Catch people doing something right,' says Paul. A quote widely attributed to C. S. Lewis expresses it perfectly: 'Considering others better than yourself is not about thinking less of yourself, but thinking of yourself less.' How can I help others?

Have you heard the story about the man who had been on a desert island? He had been shipwrecked, and he spent about seven years on the island. Eventually, when a passing liner saw him, they sent a small boat to rescue him. They realized that he had survived very well eating the fruit on the island and using the wood. He had constructed for himself three shelters covered with palm leaves. The rescue team said, 'Three shelters for one man?' And he said, 'That's the shelter I sleep in.' And they said, 'Well, what's that?' He said, 'That's the church where I worship.' 'And the other?' 'Well, that's the church I used to go to.' We know sometimes that happens, and I want you to hear my heart very carefully here. There are times when division is part of God's bigger plan. If you look in history, I think one of the great divides was the Protestant Reformation. God was at work in that movement at a very important time in the history of the church. But more often than not, the issues that we split and divide over are usually down to selfish ambition and vain conceit. There are times when, for the sake of the gospel, the truth about Jesus and those essentials that we commit and adhere to, we do have to part company. But those occasions are few and far between, and before we take that kind of stand, we need to make sure our heart is right and our motives are clear.

Look at Jesus

Let's look at this final part, verses 5–11. I wonder if in your Bible verses 5–11 are set out differently on the page? They are set out like a quote, because Paul here is probably quoting a first-century hymn. It was a confession, what we would call today a creed, the truth about Jesus set to music. And it is quite important that we sing good theology, because what we sing we tend to believe, and the good things we believe we tend to sing. That's why lyrics of songs and hymns are very important. Under the inspiration of the Holy Spirit, Paul takes up a well-known hymn or song sung within the first-century church, and he applies it to his friends at Philippi. Look at yourself, look at others, but most of all – look at Jesus.

If you want to think about getting along together, of selflessness, of thinking less about yourself and more about others, then think about Jesus. You see this first-century equivalent of Stuart Townend had penned something which tells us about our Lord Jesus. It talks about the position Jesus *held* (verse 6), 'who, being in very nature God, did not consider equality with God something to be used to his own advantage'. That was the position that Jesus held. Then we read the position that Jesus *took* in verses 7 and 8:

> He made himself nothing
>> by taking the very nature of a servant,
>> being made in human likeness.
> And being found in appearance as a man,
>> he humbled himself
>> by becoming obedient to death –
>>> even death on a cross!

'He made himself nothing' – he emptied himself. He didn't empty himself of his divinity, his divine form, his equality with God, but he surrendered his divine rights and cloaked his divine glory and became human in the form of a slave. Paul stops his friends in their tracks and he says, 'Think for a moment about Jesus.' Even though in very nature God, he didn't cling on to that, but was willing to lay aside the glory of heaven and come to earth, to the most humble of circumstances, and his obedience led him to the most ignominious death that anyone could think of. Why? Because he loved us.

We've looked at the position Jesus *held*, the position Jesus *took*, and now he writes about the position Jesus *has*. He says in verse 9, 'Therefore God exalted him', literally 'highly exalted him'. 'God highly exalted him to the highest place.'

> And gave him the name that is above every name,
> that at the name of Jesus every knee should bow,
>   in heaven and on earth and under the earth,
> and every tongue acknowledge that Jesus Christ is Lord,
>   to the glory of God the Father.

Verses 9–11 anticipate the end of the age. They anticipate the coronation of King Jesus, when every knee shall bow and every tongue confess that Jesus Christ is Lord, to the glory of God the Father. What an amazing confession. It is one of the finest passages of Christology that we have in the New Testament. It's astonishing. Many theologians have speculated on what it meant for Jesus to 'empty' himself. In what sense did he empty himself? How much of his God-ness was laid aside? But friends, these verses are meant to lead us to wonder and worship. That's why Paul includes them here.

As wonderful as these verses are, this piece of sublime theology, written as a confession to inspire wonder and worship, is used by Paul in the real world of prickly people and sticky relationships. Paul is saying, 'As you sing, Philippian church, about the wonder of the incarnation, the glory of salvation in Christ, and look forward to the consummation of the age when Jesus shall be declared Lord, to the glory of God the Father, just remember how you talk about your sister or brother at the end of the benediction, how you treat them when you are in a church meeting, or what you say about them behind their backs.'

You see, friends, this is applied theology. All of theology needs to be applied. This is about the real world of relationships. And in your community there are people who are broken, people who are lost, and we've got to learn how we can work together. What hope can we offer to a divided world if, when they come into the church, they find a divided community of people who profess to know Jesus? The world has got enough fractured relationships. What the world needs is grace, and the one who gives that grace is the one who gave himself for us.

Some years ago I was visiting a friend. We were working together on a writing project, and one evening my friend said, 'You can take this evening off, Ian, because I've got to speak at a missions conference.' And I said, 'Well, I'll come with you. I'll come and support you.' And we drove off to a church on the other side of the city, and when we walked into the lobby, there was the most huge bronze sculpture cast that I had ever seen. It's the work of an American artist called Max Greiner, and that particular statue is commemorating Jesus washing Peter's feet (John 13).

But in this particular church it is twice life-size. So, as you walk into the main entranceway of the church, this bronze cast stands right in front of you. Immediately, being a pastor and a practical sort of guy, I thought, 'Who on earth put that there?' If you've got a wheelchair-user or a mum who is pushing a stroller or a buggy, they are going to have to walk right the way round that. And when it comes to fellowship time and breaking out for coffee, or wanting to have small prayer groups, this thing is right in the middle. Then it dawned on me: they had put it there on purpose because it was their mission statement. It was so big, you couldn't avoid it. You had to walk round it. And every Sunday and through the week as the various youth activities, children's activities, the committees and the boards of elders met, as they walked into the main lobby, they were reminded that Jesus took a towel and a bowl, and he bent down and washed the feet of his disciples, including Judas, and said, 'I'm your Lord, your Master, and if I've done this for you, then you should do as I have done.'

Friends, this evening, whatever the state of your church at the moment, what it needs are men and women who live the Jesus way, who do the Jesus things and love one another because Jesus loved us.

Wanted – Faithful Gospel Workers

by Ruth Padilla DeBorst

Ruth Padilla DeBorst has been involved in leadership development and theological education for integral mission in her native Latin America for many years now. She currently serves as Director of Christian Formation and Leadership Development with World Vision International. She sits on the board of the Latin American Theological Fellowship and of INFEMIT (The International Fellowship for Mission Transformation). She lives in Costa Rica, where she shares parenting of their blended, multi-cultural family with her husband, James Padilla DeBorst, and community life with the members of Casa Adobe.

Wanted – Faithful Gospel Workers: Philippians 2:12–30

Brief moments ago, I was on my phone, texting back and forth with our youngest daughter, who is currently in the US visiting a couple of her sisters. For those of us who grew up without the internet or cellular phones, this direct access to people across the world and many time zones away is still pretty amazing. I keenly remember the days in which my dad's letters during his travels arrived even after he did! And many of you surely knew missionary service terms that lasted many years, because travel took so long and was so expensive and risky that it would not be undertaken too often.

Imagine, then, what it meant for Paul and his mission companions to travel around the coastal areas of the Mediterranean in the first century. No GPS, radars or satellites to guide ships and alert to storms. No means of communication as we know them. Travel was an extremely demanding and life-threatening business. Travellers were subject to the vagaries of weather and vulnerable to abusive sailors and bandits.

In today's passage we encounter three men who braved storms, illness and threats of all sorts in their efforts to encourage and serve the budding Christian communities in the heartlands of the Roman Empire. Although they lived in times and places so distant from ours, we can learn much from their examples as faithful gospel workers, and yet more from the nature of the relationships they have with one another and with the churches in which they minister.

The gospel workers

Let's begin with Epaphroditus. Paul does not need to introduce him to the faithful in Philippi, because they know him well. He is one of them. Turn to Philippians 2:25–30:

> But I think it is necessary to send back to you Epaphroditus, my brother, co-worker and fellow soldier, who is also your messenger, whom you sent to take care of my needs. For he longs for all of you and is distressed because you heard he was ill. Indeed he was ill, and almost died. But God had mercy on him, and not on him only but also on me, to spare me sorrow upon sorrow. Therefore I am all the more eager to send him, so that when you see him again you may be

glad and I may have less anxiety. So then, welcome him in the Lord with great joy, and honour people like him, because he almost died for the work of Christ. He risked his life to make up for the help you yourselves could not give me.

From the passage, we gather that Epaphroditus had originally been sent by them to Paul for two purposes: to carry their gift to Paul and to accompany him in difficult times. Travel in precarious conditions had taken a toll, however, and Ephaphroditus had become so ill that he had almost died. Happily, God had spared his life, and he was now returning with this very letter in hand. Again, his trip had a couple of purposes: to convey Paul's letter, and to reassure his community of his restored health.

'Why would Paul send him on yet another gruelling trip if his health has been so frail?' some of the recipients of the letter might wonder. 'Had he done something wrong?' 'Had Paul tired of his presence?' Paul makes sure all doubts are dispelled through words of commendation. He calls Epaphroditus 'my brother, co-worker and fellow soldier'. He emphasizes the bond the Spirit had woven between them. He and Epaphroditus are as family to each other. They are also joined in ministry, and they share the privilege of struggling and suffering for their faith. Epaphroditus had grown to become extremely dear to him, and yet Paul is willing to release him. He is eager to let him go back to his people so that they too may benefit from his presence.

The other gospel worker mentioned is Timothy. Verses 19–24:

> I hope in the Lord Jesus to send Timothy to you soon,
> that I also may be cheered when I receive news about you.
> I have no one else like him, who will show genuine concern
> for your welfare. For everyone looks out for their own
> interests, not those of Jesus Christ. But you know that
> Timothy has proved himself, because as a son with his
> father he has served with me in the work of the gospel.
> I hope, therefore, to send him as soon as I see how things
> go with me. And I am confident in the Lord that I myself
> will come soon.

Paul again identifies the bond between them as a familial one. While Paul alludes to Epaphroditus as a brother, most likely because of his age, he refers to Timothy as a son. Paul upholds Timothy as worthy of special mention, as one who has worked closely alongside him and shares his vision of ministry. Yet what makes him worthy of praise is not, in Paul's view, that he is a great public speaker, an astounding miracle worker or a crowd-drawing star. No! What Paul highlights is the fact that Timothy shows genuine concern for the welfare of the believers, instead of focusing on his own interests. This is what makes him worthy of Paul's highest recommendation.

The third leader is Paul himself. He describes himself as being poured out like a drink offering on their behalf. His life, as he has already told them, does not belong to him, but rather to Christ and to them. This brings him joy, even in the midst of suffering, and should encourage the Philippians in the midst of the challenges they face.

Their lives and relationships

Now we ask, what do Epaphroditus, Timothy and Paul have in common? Why might Paul dedicate such a long portion of his letter to talking about them? And what might their lives and relationships reveal to us about what it means to live as faithful gospel workers?

From the very beginning of the letter, Paul has been exhorting the followers of Jesus to live in a way worthy of the gospel. In other words, to lead lives that attest to the good news of God's reconciling love in the world, to go against the grain of our self-seeking and self-promoting world, and to be willing to die as Jesus did. Yet further – and perhaps more difficult than some glorious martyr death that would record one's name in history – be willing to *live* as Jesus did, putting others before self and striving for the unity of the community.

What these three men have in common is precisely their *other-centred* posture in life. Their top priority is not their own advantage, but the benefit of others. They are willing to sacrifice their personal well-being for the sake of building up the community. This makes them faithful witnesses of the good news of God's love, not only in word, but also in attitude and in action. It is precisely because these men exhibit the Christ-like, *other-centred* attitude which Paul has been seeking to inspire in the growing community of Jesus' followers in Philippi, and they act accordingly, that he upholds them as examples of faithful gospel workers.

For Paul, this is a straightforward issue. The only way you will make the good news known, he assures the Philippians, is if you live it out as a community. There is no space for grumbling, arguing, competing or building oneself up at the cost of others. Your salvation will be made evident in the way you live together. So yet more significant than the individual performance even of these faithful workers is the nature of the relationship between them and with the churches with which they minister.

Epaphroditus, Timothy and Paul are not simply thrown together by force of chance or personal preference. They are bound to one another by their relationship to Christ Jesus and by the work of the Spirit. And these bonds are made visible in that they are now like family to one another. Paul says, 'Epaphroditus, my brother . . . Timothy, my son'.

So also are they tied into the church body in Philippi. God's reconciling work through Christ brings them together, in spite of all the external and internal factors conspiring against their unity. In Paul's words, 'It is God who works in you to will and to act in order to fulfil his good purpose' (Philippians 2:13). It is God who is weaving them together as a body. These bonds created by God are at the core of their joint ministry, their joint suffering and their joint witness. These bonds create a sending community and a receiving community. Because of these bonds, what happens to Paul in prison in Rome, and what happens to Epaphroditus' health, matter to the community of believers in Philippi. The communities of Jesus' followers strewn across the Roman Empire are not separated by seas, no matter how risky crossing them might be. Neither are they joined by Roman roads, no matter how supposedly peaceful they are. They are held together only by God.

As Paul also reminded the Christians scattered around Asia Minor,

> You are no longer foreigners and strangers, but fellow citizens with God's people and also members of his household, built on the foundation of the apostles and prophets, with Christ Jesus himself as the chief cornerstone. In him the whole building is joined together and rises to become a holy temple in the Lord. And in him you too are being built together to become a dwelling in which God lives by his Spirit.
> (Ephesians 2:19–22)

God makes his presence known in the gathering of all those who allow themselves to be woven together by his Spirit. It is only where people are living together as one that God is present. Church buildings, religious hierarchy and doctrinal packages do not guarantee God's presence. It is the gathering of God's people that constitutes God's temple; it is in the community itself that God makes his presence known through the Spirit.

Our response

The last question we had asked was: what might the lives and relationships of these first-century followers of Jesus reveal to us about what it means to live as faithful gospel workers today?

We too, followers of Jesus around the globe, are woven together by God's reconciling love. Much as our world would classify us according to social status, colour, nationality and ethnicity, and would build separation walls of indifference, prejudice and antagonism, the Spirit's work makes us one. And as much as the global consumer market seeks to superficially unify our tastes, values, styles and aspirations, it is not globalization that brings us together, but the Spirit who makes us one.

Truly, each and every one of us is called to faithful service in the particular families, neighbourhoods, jobs and societies in which God has put us. Yet faithful testimony of the good news is not the single-handed affair of some heroic individual missionary. It is a community affair only fully carried out by a body of people woven together by Christ's reconciling work.

Does that mean there is no place for individual callings, vocations and ministries? By no means! The Spirit has gifted each and every one of God's children with a unique blend of gifts and talents, passions and skills to be put to the service of God's mission. Life will take us all on different paths, with particular joys and challenges, and we must each grapple with discerning God's calling in the midst of them. At the same time, we have to recognize that we have been made by and for community.

You see, much as theologians through the years have attempted to describe God with abstract, individual and absolute attributes, God's self-revelation makes God known as the Being-in-relation. Father, Son and Holy Spirit interact in an ever-mutual love relationship that binds them as one God. Father, Son and Holy Spirit respond to one another in love because God is love. This love is not some ethereal, unsubstantial, emotional state. It takes on concrete expression in mutual submission, service and unified action in God's world. And it becomes most dramatically visible when God, Creator and Sustainer of all life, breaks into history, squeezes into human skin, hangs out with those considered least, takes on human pain and limitation, humiliation and death for confronting the powers that are choking people, and finally rises to new life and loving reign. This is the story we are all created to be a part of.

When God chose to mark humanity with God's image, the Spirit rooted God's communal identity at the core of our being. We too are able to respond in love to one another. And full realization as human beings is found, not in reaching the highest individual achievement, as our deadening consumer society would make us believe, but in being bound in love to God, to one another, and to the rest of creation. Again, that love is not some ethereal, unsubstantial emotional state that ebbs and flows with waves of convenience or desire, but a radical commitment of mutual submission, service and unified action in God's world. A love historically embodied with all its social, political, economic and ecological outworkings. The sort of love that moved the church in Philippi to respond financially to Paul's need, the sort of love that will not tolerate superfluous spending in one corner of the global church while people are dying of hunger in another.

The community woven together by the Spirit, in the words of Walsh and Keesmaat, 'is a community in which the word of Christ dwells richly. A community that is shaped as a countercultural force through the subversive worship of a subversive Lord.'[1]

The presence of Christ's Word in the Christian community nurtures an alternative worldview from that of the dominant culture. According to this renewed worldview, it is not the powers of the market that pull all the strings. Jesus is Lord even over the global market. Only he is worthy of worship – no matter what the imperial decree of the day may order.

This community has made a radical choice for a hospitable inclusion that stands in challenging opposition to the class, ethnic, linguistic, gender categories in which our world slots people in order to discriminate against some and favour others. This choice is possible because the members of this community are so fully aware of their personal sin and insufficiency that they hold no grounds for judgment of others. They recognize they are sustained only by grace and not by religious appearance.

The mobility this community promotes is not the upward one, which reduces other people to rungs in a stepping ladder towards the top. The movement this community strives for is a descending one, modelled after the God who became human and experienced the darkest depths of death for love's sake. This movement takes concrete shape not only in distant charity, but in radical divestment and redistribution of wealth and opportunity.

The leadership bred in this community is not the self-seeking protagonism of stardom so common in the political, social and even religious scene. Leadership is measured, rather, in terms of service, and modelled after the Master who – contrary to all social and cultural expectations – washed his disciples' feet.

The scope of influence of this community is not the narrow realm of internal church business. The agenda it pursues is nothing less than God's all-encompassing recon-ciliation of all things through his Son. It plunges Jesus' followers into the messiness of peacemaking and earth-keeping. The entire world is its arena, because the whole world belongs to God.

And it is in this broad, messy, broken and beautiful world that God so loves that we are called to live out God's mission as a community of faithful witnesses of the good news of God's upside-down kingdom.

Notes

1. Brian Walsh and Sylvia Keesmaat, *Colossians Remixed: Subverting the Empire* (InterVarsity Press, 2004), p. 200.

Profit and Loss: Philippians 3:1–16

by Ian Coffey

This is the second of the evening addresses that Ian gave in week 2, continuing the series in the letter to the Philippians.

Profit and Loss: Philippians 3:1–16

Let me ask you a question: In your church does your minister, vicar, pastor or lay preacher ever say in the course of a sermon, 'finally' and then carry on for about another twenty minutes? Hands up if that is true in your church. Do you know, when we are teaching people to preach, why we get them to do that? It is to give you hope. That is the only reason. Hope that the end is in sight.

What has that got to do with our passage? Well, if you look at chapter 3:1, Paul in the original language uses the word 'finally', and then he carries on for another few chapters. In fact, if you look at chapter 4:8, he has another 'finally'. That's his final 'finally'. What we believe is that at this particular point in the letter Paul is preparing to finish. It is actually in his mind to conclude, and at that moment, under the inspiration and influence of the Holy Spirit, he makes a digression.

One of the things I love about Ruth, my wife, is her ability to digress. When we were first married, I confess I found it really irritating, and I would say something like, 'Look, I haven't got that long to live, just give me the headlines.' But as the years have gone by, I've discovered that her digressions are far more entertaining than where they lead to, because on the way you pick up all kinds of bits of information, and the detail, as I've learnt, is very important. Paul, under the influence of the Spirit, makes a wonderful digression, a God-given digression, because in the course of this he opens his heart and shares something of his own personal story, his passion for Christ, and these verses are a very rich part of the whole of this letter.

In verse 2 he says, 'Watch out', and he uses what we would consider to be very un-Christian language. He says, 'Watch out for those dogs, those evildoers, those mutilators of the flesh.' Now actually in the language in which he was writing or dictating this letter he doesn't just say, 'Watch out.' He says three times, 'Watch out, watch out, watch out.' Now if you are a parent or a grandparent, you will know exactly what he is doing there. He is triple-underlining something. You know those moments when you say to your children, 'Read my lips and then repeat after me what I have just said.' Three times Paul says, 'Watch out.' So what is it that leads him to this divine digression? What is he wanting to warn his friends about, and why is he using such strong language? Who are these dogs? These evildoers? These mutilators of the flesh?

In the early years this young church faced all kinds of pressures. Pressures from the state, from a hostile culture, but also pressures that came from within the Christian family, from those wanting to add to the gospel. And one particular group were called the Judaizers or the circumcision party. They came from a very orthodox Jewish background, and as far as they were concerned, these non-Jews coming into the church, being baptized and accepted was just a step too far. The party line they took was: 'You actually need to become more of a Jew in order to become a proper Christian.' So, if you are a man, you need to be circumcised, you need to observe the Sabbaths and the festivals, you need to eat only kosher food and you need to adhere to the customs and traditions of the elders. And Paul became one of the great opponents of that view, because he saw that what they were trying to do was to add to the gospel of the saving grace of God in the person of Jesus.

And, actually, when you look through the history of the church over 2,000 years, false teaching, heresy, cults always have the same message: 'Jesus is not enough.' It is Jesus plus: Jesus plus this special revelation, Jesus plus this extra experience. But Paul, Peter, James and John fearlessly proclaimed that the good news is that there is no other name given under heaven by which we must be saved. Only Jesus is able to bring us into a right relationship with God.

Why the language? Well, Paul is actually playing with words, because a Jew, an orthodox Jew in particular, would refer to Gentiles as 'dogs'. One famous rabbi was asked, 'If God doesn't like Gentiles, why did he make so many of them?' To which he answered, 'to fuel the fires of hell'. That was the sense of chauvinism that was there. Paul is saying that these people who regard the non-Jew as a dog are finding themselves outside of God's grace. These are the people who actually do evil. Why? Because they are adding to the gospel; they are putting obstacles in the way of men and women finding freedom and forgiveness in Jesus because of his death on the cross. He calls them 'mutilators of the flesh'; he doesn't even use the proper word for circumcision, because he said they are focusing on all the wrong issues, and this is what causes him to break off into this divine digression. A word of warning, he says, 'Don't let anybody trip you up. Don't let anybody tell you that the message you have received is not enough, that something else needs to be added.' And he goes on to share something of his story.

A man with a past

We have three phases of his story in these verses. First of all, he says, 'I'm a man with a past' (verses 4–6). He says, 'These people boast in what they are confident in. But actually the true circumcision are those who worship by the Sprit of God, who glory in Jesus and don't put any confidence in their human achievements or attainments.' And then he indulges in a little bit of rhetoric. He says, 'Actually, if we are going to talk about confidence, if we are going to compare people's bloodlines and their pedigree, let me tell you about myself.'

And you will know, if you have read the story contained in the book of Acts, Doctor Luke's account of the growth of the early church, that the conversion of Saul of Tarsus is an astonishing story. Saul, an orthodox Jew, hated those who went around saying Jesus, the crucified carpenter from Nazareth, was the Messiah, and he did all that he could to oppose them. He was so incensed that he got letters of authority from the ruling elite, set off from Jerusalem to Damascus, and he had one thing in view – to get these people off the face of the earth, to throw them into prison, to persecute them until they recanted of what he saw as heresy. And on the road to Damascus, Saul of Tarsus meets the risen Jesus.

But up until that point, if you had asked Saul, 'What makes you right with God?', he would have said, 'Three specific things: my race, my religion and my righteousness'. 'My race – I was circumcised on the eighth day.' That was the traditional time when a baby boy would be circumcised. 'I'm of the people of Israel, I'm of the tribe of Benjamin, a Hebrew of Hebrews, even named after King Saul. If we are going to boast about our status and our pedigree, that's my bloodline.' Then he says, 'My religion: I was a Pharisee.' The word 'Pharisee' means 'the separated ones'. From a very early age he had decided he wanted to study the Law, the Torah and the Prophets. He studied under probably the greatest theologian of his day, a man called Gamaliel. He knew vast chunks of the Old Testament Scriptures off by heart; he knew the traditions of the elders. He said, 'As far as I was concerned, my religion was right at the core of my being. I was confident in my race, my religion and my righteousness.' And if you are following in your Bible, you will see different translations bring out that legalistic righteousness, or righteousness according to the law. Paul was somebody who wanted to keep every last jot of the law, to make sure that he was living a blameless, faultless life.

One of the questions that we sometimes get asked is: 'Don't all religions ultimately lead to God? Isn't it a little bit like going up one of the peaks here in the Lake District? There are different paths that you can take, but they all lead to the same summit.' For those who ask that kind of question, I want to pose a question in return: 'If all roads lead to God, why on earth would God want to convert Saul of Tarsus?' He was a man steeped in religion who sought to live a righteous life according to the legal code. But you see, what Saul of Tarsus discovered on the road to Damascus was that all of this was not enough to make unholy people right with a holy God. All the religion in the world, all the legalistic righteousness, all of that spiritual pedigree that Saul of Tarsus was proud of, none of that can deal with the core issue: the issue of a fallen and depraved, sinful human heart.

A man with a present

But then Paul writes on in the next verses and talks about the present: he was a man with a present. I don't know whether you can see in your Bible, but it is quite clear in mine, that up until now, talking about his past, it is all about 'me, me, me'. But now, from verses 7–11, it is all about Jesus. The name Jesus or Christ or the pronoun occurs nine times. And actually that is a picture of what happened. Paul's confidence shifted entirely from his race, his religion and his legalistic righteousness to Jesus, to Christ alone.

Look at the language that he uses as he talks about how Jesus now fills his horizon completely. Verse 7 says, 'Whatever were gains to me [or to my profit] I now consider loss.' That's the language of accountancy. My race, my religion, my righteousness which I thought were in my profit column, actually, when I met Jesus on the road to Damascus, I saw that they belonged in the loss column. And then in verse 8 he says, 'I consider them garbage.' The translators of the NIV are being very polite. That isn't the word Paul uses. He uses the word 'excrement'. The things that I trusted in, in God's sight, are just filthy rags; they are not sufficient to make me right with God; they can't put right that moral dilemma within me, that spiritual lostness, the depravity caused by sin.

In verses 8–9 he says, 'I consider them garbage, that I may gain Christ and be found in him, not having a right-eousness of my own that comes from the law but that which is through faith in Christ – the righteousness that comes from God on the basis of faith.' We call it 'imputed righteousness'. All the goodness, the righteousness of Jesus, the Holy One of God, the sin-bearer who had lived a sinless life, all of his righteousness placed to your account. You are not only forgiven; you are declared righteous in the presence of a holy God. Do you flinch a little when we sing that great hymn of Charles Wesley, when we come to the last verse: 'Bold I approach the eternal throne'?[1] And you think, 'I'm not sure that I feel that bold, because I'm not the best parent in the world, I don't always tell the truth and I haven't always got a handle on my tongue or on my temper.' Friend, understand this: that boldness is not down to how good you are, but how good Jesus is. That is the source of your confidence. I'm not righteous; I can't do it, but Jesus has done it, and there is one who stands in heaven for you and me and pleads our cause. The Father looks on him and accredits his righteousness to you and to me.

Look at verse 10, passionate words: 'I want to know Christ – yes, to know the power of his resurrection and participation in his sufferings.' Paul is saying, 'When I realized what Jesus had accomplished on the cross, when the curtain in the temple was torn in two, from the top to the bottom, I realized that the only way was being made wide open, and that all of the race and religious accreditation in the world wouldn't make me right with God. But there is one who has gone through the curtain, bearing his own blood, and because of Jesus, I can be made right with God.' Paul says, 'That is why I want to know the power of his resurrection and share in his sufferings, because now it is not all about me; it is all about him.'

Some of you may have been a little bit perturbed at verse 11 when Paul says, 'So, *somehow*, attaining to the resurrection from the dead'. Is he doubting, in his Roman prison cell awaiting trial before Caesar? Is there some kind of turmoil within his spirit? No – this is the language of worship. This is the language of wonder and adoration. John Newton, who wrote, amongst other great hymns, 'Amazing Grace, How Sweet the Sound' and 'How Sweet the Name of Jesus Sounds in a Believer's Ear', often used to say, 'When I get to heaven, there will be three wonders. I will wonder at those who are there that I didn't think would be there. I will wonder at those who are not there that I thought would be there, but the greatest wonder of all will be that I am there.' That is what Paul is saying. The man who stood giving approval to the death of Stephen, the first Christian martyr, the man who persecuted the church, says, '*Somehow* even I, the least of the apostles, the chief of sinners, *somehow* even I can know that welcome and embrace of the Father.'

I want to ask you tonight, are you sure of that relationship? Are you sure that your sins are forgiven, that if tonight God called you from this life to the next, that you have a place in heaven secured for you on the basis of what Christ has done? You sometimes meet folk who say, 'I've been involved with this church for X numbers of years; I've held this post; I've held this position; I come to Keswick. I sing as loudly as anybody else; I give; I'm one of the first to put my hand up to volunteer.' All of those things are wonderful and commendable, but do you know tonight that Jesus Christ is your Saviour and your Lord? My hope is not in my denomination, not in the things that I've done, not in the offices that I have held, not even in the study and the letters after my name; it is in Christ alone.

If you are not sure about that, can I ask you tonight to talk to somebody in your family, in your church party, one of our prayer team here? Just seal that in your heart with God. Some of you I know are saying, 'I don't feel I'm good enough.' Well done, you've qualified; you are absolutely right, you are not. Jesus has done it all. Amazing grace. Actually, it's not amazing grace; it is more than that: it's outrageous that we should be loved by the Father and saved by the Son and indwelt by the Spirit.

A man with a future

Paul was a man with a past, a man with a present, and he was a man with a future. Just remember for a moment as we read these last verses, Paul is writing to some friends who, as we said the other evening, were discouraged and dry, and there was this threat of disunity. Imagine what an inspiration this was for them to hear read aloud the testimony of Paul, their founding pastor. They had heard him tell the story of what Jesus had done in his life before, but here he was telling them again what Christ had done, and they can hear that note of passion. Prison hasn't made him stale. He hasn't gone off the boil. In fact, they can feel, through these words, the throbbing intensity of somebody who is pressing on with God.

Look at what he says in verse 12: 'Not that I have already obtained all this.' He says, 'I haven't arrived yet; I haven't yet been made perfect; there is still new territory for me to explore. There is fresh ground for me to discover.' Verses 13–14: 'Forgetting what is behind and straining towards what is ahead, I press on towards the goal to win the prize for which God has called me heavenwards in Christ Jesus.' Paul says, 'forgetting what is behind', not in any sense rubbishing that, but saying, 'I don't want to dwell on that. I press on, to lay hold of that for which Christ Jesus lay hold of me. I'm pressing on with God.' Verse 13: 'One thing I do' – that is how the translators have put it. Actually in verse 13 he says, 'one thing' – the translators have added the verb 'I do'. 'One thing,' he says, 'I want to be single-minded; I want to be single-focused; I want to press on with God.'

I remember years ago when Ruth and I went to Bulgaria in Eastern Europe. I've always felt uncomfortable with phrases like 'senior citizens' – it just doesn't sound right, does it? But in Bulgaria they've got this lovely phrase: they talk about 'those born early'. Well, for those of you who were born early, can I plead with you? Show us how to finish well. Show us how to cross the line running. Show us what it means to be men and women of faith. We read about 'sell-by' dates and 'use–by' dates, but God doesn't believe in 'sell-by' or 'use–by' dates – hallelujah! You may have reached a point where you can't do all the things that you did, but don't fall into the trap of using that horrible phrase: 'It's someone else's turn.' What does that mean? Someone else's turn to follow Jesus? No. And some of you 'born-early' saints, show us how to cross the finish line running. 'Ian,' you say, 'how?' Let me give you three things.

Number one: passion. Passion for Jesus, a passion for Jesus that is infectious. The kind of passion for Jesus that spreads contagion everywhere. Second word: prayer. One of the greatest things that you can contribute to the life of your church is to pray for your leaders, for those who lead worship, for those who open God's Word, for those in your community who have yet to meet Jesus, for those who are new in their faith. You could be coming into the most important phase of your ministry, a ministry of prayer. Passion, prayer, and the third word? Praise. I don't know whether you remember Victor Meldrew on the television. I think he belongs to quite a few churches. Sometimes when Ruth catches me getting a little bit grumpy, she won't call me Ian. She calls me 'Vic'. And I know exactly what she is saying. I agree with you, things are not like they used to be. Sometimes things are certainly not as good as they used to be, but why not allow your words to be positive and affirming. Praise, encourage, thank, bless. When an older saint does that kind of thing, you don't know how much strength that gives. That is what Paul is doing here. He knows his friends are finding the pressure great, so what does he do? He gives an example of a Christian who is finishing the race well.

My parents, both with the Lord now, were passionate about Keswick and the message of Keswick. When my mum went to be with the Lord about seven or eight years ago, at the funeral her pastor, in giving a tribute to her, said, 'They don't make many like Elsie any more.' Friends, let's aim for people to say that about you and me at the thanksgiving service. Not 'Thank goodness they've gone', but, 'They lived well and they left an example for us to follow.'

Ruth and I went to a church last year where a lovely couple in their nineties had both died within the space of a few days of each other. The pastor shared the news with the congregation that Sunday morning. He mentioned their names, and he gave a list of all the things they had done since that church was first planted. Then he said, 'When our friends went to be with Jesus this week, they left behind two pairs of very big shoes. Who is going to fill them?' Let them say that about us, friends. Run the race well, cross the line, accelerating over those final yards.

Many of you will know of Amy Carmichael. She had a few days' break one year in the mountains in Switzerland, not far from where Ruth and I lived for a number of years, and she saw a freshly turned grave and a headstone that had obviously been planted very recently. It belonged to a Swiss mountain guide who had been leading a party, but there had been an avalanche, and he had been killed in the disaster. But it was the inscription that caught her eye. It had the man's name, his date of birth, his date of death, but the epitaph simply said, 'He died climbing.' She went back to her hotel room and she wrote this poem:

Make us Thy mountaineers;
We would not linger on the lower slope,
Fill us afresh with hope, oh God of Hope,
That undefeated we may climb the hill
As seeing Him who is invisible.

Let us die climbing. When this little while
Lies far behind us, and the last defile
Is all alight, and in that light we see
Our Leader and our Lord – what will it be?[2]

Let us die climbing. That was Paul's testimony, and notice in those last two verses he says, 'All of us, then, who are mature should take such a view of things. And if on some point you think differently, that too God will make clear to you' (verse 15). He is saying, 'Friends, come on, let's live up to what we've already attained. Let's live up to the calling we have in Christ. Let's run the race with our eyes fixed on Jesus.'

Notes

1. Charles Wesley, 'And Can It Be that I Should Gain?' (1738).
2. 'The Last Defile' by Amy Carmichael in *Toward Jerusalem* (CLC Ministries, 1989).

Keswick 2014

Keswick Convention 2014 Bible Readings, Evening Celebrations and Lectures available free on www.keswickministries.org
Listen or download the mp3

Keswick Convention 2014 teaching from Essential Christian
All Bible readings and talks recorded at Keswick 2014 are available now on CD, DVD*, MP3 download and USB stick from www.essentialchristian.com/keswick.

Keswick teaching available as an MP3 download
Just select the MP3 option on the teaching you want, and after paying at the checkout your computer will receive the teaching MP3 download – now you can listen to teaching on the go: on your iPod, MP3 player or even your mobile phone.

Over fifty years of Keswick teaching all in one place
Visit www.essentialchristian.com/keswick to browse Keswick Convention Bible teaching as far back as 1957! You can also browse albums by worship leaders and artists who have performed at Keswick, including Stuart Townend, Keith and Kristyn Getty, plus Keswick Live albums and the Precious Moments collection of DVDs.

To order, visit www.essentialchristian.com/keswick or call 0845 607 1672

* Not all talks are available on DVD.

KESWICK MINISTRIES

The vision of Keswick Ministries is *the spiritual renewal of God's people for his mission in today's world.*

We are committed to the deepening of the spiritual life in individuals and church communities through the careful exposition and application of Scripture, with the following priorities:

Lordship of Christ: to encourage submission to the lordship of Christ in all areas of personal and corporate living.

Transformation by Word and Spirit: to encourage active obedience to God's Word through a dependency upon the indwelling and fullness of the Holy Spirit for life transformation and effective living.

Evangelism and mission: to provoke a strong commitment to evangelism and mission in the British Isles and worldwide.

Whole-life discipleship: to stimulate the discipling and training of people of all ages in godliness, service and sacrificial living, equipping them to participate in the mission of God in every area of life.

Unity and family: to provide a practical demonstration of evangelical unity across denominations and across generations.

Keswick Ministries seeks to achieve its aims by:

- sustaining and developing the three-week summer Convention in Keswick UK, teaching and training Christians of all ages and backgrounds;
- providing training for preachers, leaders and youth and children's workers in different parts of the UK;
- strengthening the network of 'Keswick' events in towns and cities around the UK;
- producing and promoting resources (books, DVDs and downloads, as well as TV and radio programmes) so that Keswick's teaching ministry is brought to a wider audience around the world;
- providing a year-round residential centre in Keswick for the use of church groups and Christian organizations;
- encouraging an international movement by building relationships with the many 'Keswicks' around the world, thereby seeking to strengthen local churches in their life and mission.

For further information, please see our website: www.keswickministries.org or contact our office:

Email: info@keswickministries.org
Tel: 01768 780075
Mail: Keswick Ministries, Convention Centre, Skiddaw Street, Keswick CA12 4BY, England

THE WHOLE OF LIFE
for CHRIST

DISCIPLESHIP IS ABOUT FOLLOWING JESUS AND LEARNING FROM HIM. But who is the Jesus we follow and what can we expect to learn from him? Hebrews 1 describes him as the Creator, Sustainer and ultimate heir of everything that exists! Following and learning from him will therefore impact on every aspect of how we live in the world, rather than having implications only for those parts of life which we have come to see as 'spiritual', such as church involvement, quiet times or evangelism. In Keswick 2015 we will grapple with the challenge of living the whole of life for Christ: our work, our leisure, our place in the community, our homes, our role in public life, our responsibility to care for creation, and so much more. This whole-life vision of discipleship will give us a liberating perspective that transforms our work into worship and brings Christian faith out of our church buildings and onto the streets of everyday life.

WEEK 1 **11-17 JULY** John Risbridger
WEEK 2 **18-24 JULY** Paul Mallard
WEEK 3 **25-31 JULY** Liam Goligher

VISIT WWW.KESWICKMINISTRIES.ORG

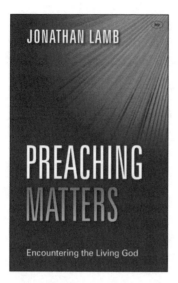

Preaching Matters

*Encountering
the Living God*
Jonathan Lamb

ISBN: 978-1-78359-149-7
192 pages, paperback

Preaching matters. It is a God-ordained means of encountering Christ. This is happening all around the world. The author recalls the student who, on hearing a sermon about new life in Christ, found faith which changed his life and future forever; and the couple facing the trauma of the wife's terminal illness who discovered that Christ was all they needed, following a sermon on Habakkuk.

When the Bible is faithfully and relevantly explained, it transforms hearts, understandings and attitudes, and, most of all, draws us into a living relationship with God through Christ.

This is a book to ignite our passion for preaching, whether we preach every week or have no idea how to put a sermon together. It will encourage every listener to participate in the dynamic event of God's Word speaking to his people through his Holy Spirit. God's Word is dynamite; little wonder that its effects are often dynamic.

'A book for both preachers and listeners … a fitting manifesto not just for the Keswick Convention, but for every local church.'
Tim Chester

Available from your local Christian bookshop or **www.thinkivp.com**

Keswick Study Guides by IVP

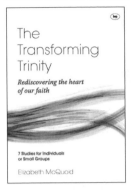

The Transforming Trinity
Rediscovering the heart of our faith
Elizabeth McQuoid

These seven studies will help you grow in your
understanding of the inexhaustible riches of the
Trinity. Find out why the Trinity is central to our
beliefs and fundamental to the working out of our
faith. Learn to worship the triune God more fully,
reflect his image more clearly, and experience
his transforming power in your life. Learn what it
really means to know the Father, follow the Son,
and walk in the Spirit. Because the Trinity is at the
heart of Christian faith and life.

'A feast for individuals and Bible study groups.'
Sam Allberry

ISBN: 978-1-84474-906-5 | 80 pages, booklet

Really?
Searching for reality in a confusing world
Elizabeth McQuoid

These seven studies help us go deeper into the truth
we are offered in Jesus Christ, and to root our lives
in it. Because Jesus offers us himself, a reality that
satisfies not only our intellectual curiosity, but also
the deepest longings of our hearts. He offers us true
security and sure hope for the future. He reshapes
our thoughts, our life, our identity and our purpose.
Real truth is found in Jesus Christ, and knowing him
changes everything.

*'Really? is a great resource to explore how the
Christian message enables us to live with real
confidence in the real world.'* Tim Chester

ISBN: 978-1-78359-158-9 | 80 pages, booklet

Available from your local Christian bookshop or **www.thinkivp.com**